Teaching the Common Core

Speaking & Listening

Standards

Strategies & Digital Tools

Kristen Swanson

EYE ON EDUCATION

Eye On Education
6 Depot Way West, Suite 106
Larchmont, NY 10538
(914) 833–0551
(914) 833–0761 fax
www.eyeoneducation.com

Library of Congress Cataloging-in-Publication Data

Swanson, Kristen.
Teaching the common core speaking and listening standards : strategies and digital tools/
by Kristen Swanson.
      pages   cm
Includes bibliographical references.
ISBN 978-1-59667-251-2
1. Oral communication—Study and teaching.
2. Listening—Study and teaching.
3. English language—Grammar—Study and teaching.
4. Language arts—Standards.
I. Title.
LB1572.S93 2013
428.0071—dc23   2013008865

10 9 8 7 6 5 4 3 2 1

Sponsoring Editor: Robert Sickles
Production Editor: Lauren Beebe
Copyeditor: Dorothy D. Anderson
Designer and Compositor: Matthew Williams, click! Publishing Services
Cover Designer: Dave Strauss, 3FoldDesign

Also Available from EYE ON EDUCATION

Professional Learning in the Digital Age:
The Educator's Guide to User-Generated Learning
Kristen Swanson

Big Skills for the Common Core:
Literacy Strategies for the 6–12 Classroom
Amy Benjamin & Michael Hugelmeyer

Common Core Literacy Lesson Plans:
Ready-to-Use Resources
Lauren Davis, Editor

Teaching Students to Dig Deeper: The Common Core in Action
Ben Johnson

The Common Core Grammar Toolkit:
Using Mentor Texts to Teach the Language Standards in Grades 3–5
Sean Ruday

Authentic Learning Experiences:
A Real-World Approach to Project-Based Learning
Dayna Laur

Vocabulary Strategies That Work: Do This—Not That!
Lori Wilfong

Teaching Critical Thinking: Using Seminars for 21st Century Literacy
Terry Roberts & Laura Billings

Writer's Workshop for the Common Core: A Step-by-Step Guide
Warren E. Combs

Rigor Is NOT a Four-Letter Word (2nd Edition)
Barbara R. Blackburn

Students Taking Charge:
Inside the Learner-Active, Technology-Infused Classroom
Nancy Sulla

About the Author

Kristen Swanson helps teachers design meaningful, interactive curricula at the local and national level. In the past she has taught at the elementary level, served as a regional consultant for Response to Intervention, and worked as an educational technology director for a public school district in Pennsylvania. She holds a B.A. degree from DeSales University, two M.A. degrees from Wilkes University, and an Ed.D. degree from Widener University. Kristen is currently an adjunct in the DeSales University instructional technology M.Ed program.

In addition to her experience as an educator, Kristen is also passionate about meaningful professional learning. She serves on the board of the Edcamp Foundation, a nonprofit organization designed to facilitate local, grassroots professional development. She has shared her ideas and expertise at an ASCD conference, TEDxPhiladelphiaEd, and Educon. She has also been published in academic journals, including *Literacy Learning: The Middle Years* and the *Journal of Reading, Writing, and Literacy*. She is also the author of *Professional Learning in the Digital Age: The Educator's Guide to User-Generated Learning*.

Kristen is active in the educational technology sphere. She is a Google Certified Teacher, Twitter Teacher, Edublog Award Nominee, and avid blogger. She strongly believes that strong curriculum fosters meaningful technology integration, and she is also interested in the learning opportunities provided by asynchronous learning.

Contents

Introduction

Speaking and listening. We do it every day for countless reasons. Routine interactions, brief exchanges, or thoughtful diatribes propel us through everything from the most mundane tasks to critical life events. Therefore, it's not surprising that speaking and listening have earned a prominent place in our K–12 standard documents, including the widely endorsed Common Core State Standards (CCSS).

The CCSS represent a national model for teaching and learning. Forty-five states and three territories have formally adopted the CCSS. Given the propensity in this country to disagree on all things surrounding public education, the popularity of these standards is amazing. After educators have spent years focusing on countless content standards, the CCSS offer a breath of fresh air. Less content is required, more emphasis is placed on process, and contrived texts are banished.

However, the speaking and listening standards endorsed by the CCSS are often neglected in K–12 schools. Many students I've informally interviewed report having to give a speech only "a few times." Coincidentally, most report being "really nervous" and "hating it." Further, observation in lots of different classrooms has led me to note that many classrooms still have more teacher talk than student talk. Teachers must revise instructional practices by adding more occasions for students to become empathetic listeners and engaging speakers.

Erik Palmer, in a recent video post about the importance of speaking well, stated, "People are realizing, when you look very closely, you'll see that you've accepted pretty mediocre speaking. And you will definitely realize that no one really teaches speaking" (Palmer, 2012). By this, Palmer means that we simply assess students on their speaking skills without giving them many opportunities to practice, observe models, or synthesize generalities.

Specifically, the Speaking and Listening Anchor Standards offer an enormous opportunity to rethink and revise current practices. They seek to deepen students' abilities to become competent, confident people. The CCSS demand explicit teaching, modeling, and practice of speaking and listening. They demand excellence. Further, the Speaking and Listening Anchor Standards explicitly state that speaking and listening should be practiced not only in language courses but in every discipline. Regardless of what you teach, you are only a few thoughtful tweaks away from emphasizing these standards without sacrificing necessary content. In fact, speaking and listening about engaging content is one of the best ways to facilitate deep, conceptual understanding. The best classrooms have significant amounts of student talk, student discussion, and student presentation. When all this is interwoven with critical reading and critical writing, it's a recipe for success.

John Hattie's research reminds teachers that feedback is one of the most powerful instructional strategies they can use in their classrooms. Emphasizing the speaking and listening standards allows teachers to leverage conversation to increase the amount of feedback provided in the classroom by teachers and peers (Hattie, 2009).

However, this book is about more than just speaking and listening in the traditional sense. It's about speaking and listening in the digital age, complete with video chats and robust networks. Clearly, today's graduates are expected to collaborate with national and international partners for both work and play. Kids need practice speaking and listening, not just face-to-face, but in digital environments.

Consider my week at work:

Monday: Videoconference with my colleague two states away
Tuesday: In-person presentation with audio, video, and a backchannel
Wednesday: Web conference with my boss to review new instructional materials
Thursday: Google+ Hangout over lunch with my sister (who lives in Greece and runs a study-abroad program)
Friday: In-person book club about instructional strategies with some teachers and principals

The integration of digital tools, conversation, and video has changed the way we behave in both social and work-related situations. Teachers need to prepare students to be competent speakers and listeners in a digital age, and the CCSS can help.

The Goal of This Text: Offering Creative Instructional Design Frameworks

This book begins with general overview information on the CCSS and the intention of a well-designed instructional framework in an effort to provide you with context and background. However, the intention of this book is to provide you with much more than context. Chapters 4 through 9 provide you with flexible instructional frameworks and digital tools aligned to every standard in the Common Core Speaking and Listening Standards. When you combine these frameworks with powerful reading and writing content from your subject area, you will see greater student engagement, comprehension, and understanding. You will also be actively preparing your students for the demands of the modern, networked world. Each design is presented with options for students at different developmental levels throughout the K–12 continuum. However, the designs recorded in this text are a starting point, not an ending point. Use your creativity to adapt and customize each learning experience for your particular group of students. There is no "wrong way" to use the resources provided in each chapter. You don't even have to read the chapters in order. Get creative and be innovative!

Various teacher perspectives will be provided at the end of each chapter. These perspectives offer practical tips and ideas based on the teachers' experiences with the frameworks. These perspectives intend to help you visualize how the frameworks could be adapted to your specific situation.

A Final Note About the Role of Transfer

To use the words of Grant Wiggins, "educational transfer is the point of education" (Wiggins, 2012). Transfer occurs when students can use information and skills you've taught them *independently* in *novel situations*. All the final assessments listed in each instructional design framework will provide students with opportunities to transfer their learning to a new situation. Although these tasks may seem different from the assessment tasks that fill most textbooks, they were designed specifically to foster high levels of rigor, engagement, and achievement. Scaffolding your lessons to promote transfer helps honor the ultimate goal of education.

If students are not transferring their learning, they are either acquiring knowledge or making meaning of it. Acquisition is the learning stage where students practice rote procedures, isolated facts, or learning recipes. Meaning making is where students generalize, synthesize, and generate insight. Both of these stages complement the role of transfer (Bransford, Brown, Cocking, Donovan, & Pellegrino, 2000).

 ## Look Back and Step Forward

By the end of this introductory chapter you should feel confident with the following concepts:

- The CCSS emphasize the need for students to speak and listen in all subject areas.
- Today's digital world means that "speaking and listening" will be an integration of face-to-face and digital formats that are both synchronous (at the same time) and asynchronous (at different times).
- This book will provide you with flexible instructional design frameworks that can be used to digitally infuse the Common Core Speaking and Listening Standards in any content area.

 ## A Question to Consider as You Reflect

How does speaking and listening help students become competent adults?

With that, you're off! You will begin your journey by exploring the general shifts within the CCSS and the competencies implied within the standards. From there, you will consider some basic principles about curriculum to help you get the most out of the instructional design frameworks in this book. Then, enjoy each instructional design framework, and be sure to share your experiences, adaptations, and successes on my blog at www.kristenswanson.org.

About the Common Core State Standards for English Language Arts

Although the focus of this text is the Common Core Standards for Speaking and Listening, a general overview of the broader Common Core Standards for English Language Arts will serve as a helpful frame of reference for you. In short, this chapter will give you the deep background knowledge required to understand the new complexities of the Common Core Speaking and Listening Standards and the instructional frameworks that follow in Chapters 4 through 10.

Common Core State Standards: What's New?

The creation of the CCSS was a state-led effort that included input from teachers, administrators, and experts. The effort was coordinated by the National Governors Association for Best Practices and the Council of Chief State School Officers. The standards were designed based upon the strongest components of existing state standards as well as cutting-edge research. They are also informed by the practices of other top-performing countries to intentionally reflect the needs of the existing global economy (National Governors Association Center for Best Practices, Council of Chief State School Officers, 2010).

Honestly, this is an incredibly exciting time in education. After years of diluting the standards at the state level in an effort to comply with the regulations of No Child Left Behind, the stakes are finally rising again. To use the words of Marzano, "All kids deserve a guaranteed and viable curriculum" (2003). The CCSS seek to provide *just that*.

Though you might be worried that the CCSS will rob you of creativity and joy in the classroom, that is not the intention of the document.

The designers of the CCSS directly state that the standards are not a curriculum. Conversely, the standards are a framework to guide teachers and schools as they construct local curricula. In their book *Understanding by Design*, Grant Wiggins and Jay McTighe (2005) compare standards and curriculum to the relationship between a building code and a blueprint in construction. All architectural designs must adhere to building codes, but the plans to build the structure are incredibly flexible. Similarly, all teachers are accountable to the CCSS, but there are innumerable ways to teach while still adhering to the standards. In short, the craft of teaching, adjusting, and designing is still intact. Phew!

Also, the authors of the CCSS have shown a strong movement away from basic acquisition. Instead of focusing on the facts and discrete qualities of literature (Really, how many syllables does a haiku have?), the CCSS focus on analysis and the derivation of meaning. For example, instead of requiring students to identify different types of figurative language (as is common in most state standard documents), the CCSS require students to "Interpret words and phrases as they are used in a text, including determining technical, connotative, and figurative meanings, and analyze how specific word choices shape meaning or tone." In many cases, the demands of the CCSS hearken back to deep comprehension or expression (National Governors Association Center for Best Practices, Council of Chief State School Officers, 2010).

In many ways, this is a huge relief as well as a call to action. Because the new standards are concise yet complex, they make it more difficult to dice learning into itty-bitty pieces. In his book *Making Learning Whole*, David Perkins referred to this syndrome as "elementitus." He states, "So troubling is this trend of approaching things through elements without the whole game in sight or a minimal presence that I like to name it as a disease: elementitus" (Perkins, 2010). Instead, a competent performance that integrates many different standards at once must be demanded; it is more holistic and representative of real life. However, facilitating this type of performance may require changes of teachers.

The movement away from recall to meaningful application of skills speaks to another dimension of the new standards. The CCSS place a strong emphasis on the cultivation of graduates who are "college and career ready." In short, this means that the goal of K–12 education is no longer a high school diploma. Regardless of whether students choose a path toward college or career, they must be able to read critically, identify bias, and solve complex problems.

Further, more and more students are entering college without the skills required to be successful. A brief by the Alliance for Education, released in May 2011, estimated costs for remedial college classes for one year at $5.6 *billion*! Such costs can be avoided if the rigor is raised in K–12 institutions.

Given the changing demands of the current knowledge-based economy, when today's kindergartners graduate, they must be ready to tackle complex problems that *may not even exist yet*. To address this need, the CCSS have a few distinct instructional shifts. Given the scope of this book and its focus on speaking and listening, we will focus on the English Language Arts (ELA) standards here.

In the English Language Arts standards, new shifts include the following:

♦ **A focus on rigorous text, especially informational text**
   The rigor of text required at each grade level within the CCSS is higher than what has been required by most states in the past. This requirement specifically addresses the declining difficulty of most educational resources, such as textbooks and trade books. Further, in 2006, Williamson found there was a significant difference between the complexity of texts required during the final year of high school and those required in the first year of college. The rigor of text demanded by the CCSS directly addresses this gap. For specifics, consider the following chart taken from Appendix A of the CCSS (National Governors Association Center for Best Practices, Council of Chief State School Officers, 2010):

Text Complexity Grade Band in the Standards	Old Lexile Ranges	Lexile Ranges Aligned to CCR Expectations
K–1	N/A	N/A
2–3	450–725	450–790
4–5	645–845	770–980
6–8	860–1010	955–1155
9–10	960–1115	1080–1305
11–CCR	1070–1220	1215–1355

The amount of informational text required by the CCSS exceeds what has been previously required by most states. Within the CCSS, seventy percent of students' readings should be informational in nature by the time they reach twelfth grade. (It's important to note that the seventy percent figure represents the percentage of informational text that students should be reading across the entire school day in all subjects, not just in the English classroom.)

♦ **An integration of literacy in science, social studies, and technical subjects**
Teaching literacy isn't just for English teachers. The official title inscribed on the Common Core Standards for ELA states, "English Language Arts and Literacy in History/Social Studies, Science, and Technical Subjects." There is collective responsibility for the cultivation of proficient speakers, readers, and writers. Within the standards, social studies teachers are encouraged to use primary sources, digital timelines, and other authentic sources. Science teachers should have students read and analyze graphs, data reports, and other scientific documents. Students must learn to read like historians and scientists. (You will notice that many of the instructional frameworks shared later in this book are highly applicable to social studies and science.)

♦ **A focus on digital media and technology**
Our students are always plugged in. Both the critical analysis and the production of media are emphasized within the Common Core Standards for ELA. This may require additional resources for schools in the United States.

♦ **Argue, argue, argue!**
By twelfth grade, only twenty percent of the writing students do in school should be geared toward sharing their personal experiences. The remaining eighty percent of their writing should be persuasive or explanatory. (Consider this: When was the last time your boss asked you to recount your vacation to Mexico? That's what I thought!) Students need to be able to explain their thinking clearly (in writing or in speech), and they need to argue big points. Argument is a theme that stretches throughout the reading, writing, and speaking demands outlined in the Common Core Standards for ELA.

♦ **Academic discussion**
Structured, academic discussion is explicitly required by the standards. Students should be able to contribute meaningfully to

conversations about complex ideas or information. Importantly, this emphasis encompasses more than traditional formal presentations. Although students certainly need to be able to share their learning in front of a prepared audience, they also need to be able to engage in the types of conversations that foster innovation, synthesis, and aha moments. Such informal conversations should be had in every classroom as part of the learning process.

Clearly, these shifts will have an impact on most classrooms. In an insightful article titled "The Common Core Ate My Baby and Other Urban Legends," Timothy Shanahan provides a warning to those who are committed to the status quo in their classrooms. He says, "Educators who shrug off these changes will face a harsh reality. The Common Core State Standards are significantly higher than what we're used to" (Shanahan, 2012, p. 10).

Therefore, it is critically important for teachers, principals, curriculum coordinators, and other school leaders to read the new standards closely, including the introductory statements and appendices. Many of the new standards are so complex that only a strategic reading will truly unearth the intention of the authors. The ELA documents currently available at www.corestandards.org include the following:

- ♦ **Common Core State Standards for English Language Arts and Literacy in History/Social Studies, Science, and Technical Subjects**
  This is the actual standards document itself, which includes grade-level indicators.
- ♦ **English Language Arts Appendix A**
  This is a summary of research supporting the key elements of the standards and a glossary of terms.
- ♦ **English Language Arts Appendix B**
  This includes text exemplars for each grade level and sample performance tasks. These tools can serve as practical jumping-off points for classroom instruction.
- ♦ **English Language Arts Appendix C**
  This appendix includes samples of student writing with comments from the authors of the standards. It provides clear examples of what success looks like when using the standards.

In a recent workshop with teachers, I provided folks with time and space to review and discuss the introduction of the Common Core Standards for

ELA. Although I was initially worried that the teachers would perceive this task as dull or irrelevant, they were incredibly grateful for the activity and the discussion that followed. One teacher came up to me after the session and said, "Thanks for making me read that. I would never have read it otherwise, and it is really important to understand where the authors of the standards are coming from. I think I get it now; we've got to change." It's important for teachers to read and talk about these documents.

Once you have explored the resources released by the authors of the CCSS, you will most likely have more questions. Luckily, there are more resources to bolster your understanding.

In addition to the standards documents themselves, many states have done substantial work unpacking and making sense of the Common Core Standards for ELA. Because the national nature of the standards allows us to leverage work done in almost any state, you may also find these resources helpful. Note that each state referenced below has used a framework analogous to the three learning stages (acquisition, meaning making, and transfer) referenced in this book.

- ◆ **Deconstructed Standards for ELA** (http://www.doe.k12.de.us/ commoncore/ela/teachertoolkit/litorg/literacy_con_reading .shtml)
  Delaware has provided daily lesson exemplars as well as a breakdown of each standard according to what students should know (acquisition), understand (meaning making), and do (transfer). This series of documents is incredibly helpful to teachers as they start to plan lessons based on the Common Core Standards for ELA.
- ◆ **Kentucky's Deconstructed Standards for ELA** (http://education .ky.gov/curriculum/ELA/Pages/ELA-Deconstructed-Standards .aspx)
  Kentucky has interpreted the standards by considering the learning targets implied by each standard at each grade level. Learning targets are broken into different categories, including knowledge (acquisition), reasoning (meaning making), performance skill (transfer), and product (transfer). This can assist teachers as they write lesson objectives or create tasks based on the standards.
- ◆ **North Carolina's Deconstructed Standards for ELA** (http:// www.dpi.state.nc.us/acre/standards/common-core-tools/)
  North Carolina has taken a slightly different approach to unpacking the standards. This document shows the general anchor

standard and the grade-level indicator side by side. North Carolina educators also created a brief narrative that explains what the standard actually *means* at that grade level. They also provided questions and prompts. These prompts can be helpful to teachers as they design tasks and lessons.

♦ **Ohio's Model Curriculum for ELA** (http://education.ohio .gov/GD/Templates/Pages/ODE/ODEDetail.aspx?Page=3& TopicRelationID=1699&Content=136734)
Ohio has created a model curriculum framework that provides teachers with enduring understandings and instructional strategies related to various subsets of the Common Core Standards for ELA. The instructional strategies are described succinctly and may prove helpful when considering your own curricular documents.

Interpreting and analyzing the CCSS is critical, and these state-level documents can provide you with different lenses through which to view the standards.

The Need for Complex Tasks and a Focus on Outputs

As educators have started to grapple with the demands of the CCSS, many new resources, questions, and concerns have arisen. I've been following the national conversation about the CCSS via conferences, social media, and academic journals. Specifically, I've noted one trend: educators are obsessed with inputs. In their fervent attempt to meet these new demands, teachers have become hyper-focused on what they are doing *as teachers.* Consider these frequent requests and resources from my Twitter feed:

♦ *I am looking for some great web 2.0 tools in order to teach the CCSS. Help!*
♦ *11 Tech Tools to Teach the Common Core State Standards. Click here!*
♦ *What teachers should do with the new CCSS . . .*

They all focus on the activities of the teacher, not the student. A true, honest focus on the demands of the new standards requires teachers to consider both what teachers do *and* what students do. Educators should focus on the outputs, not the inputs. (In the spirit of differentiation, teachers should vary the inputs based on the needs of students. Right?)

Focusing on outputs helps teachers prioritize and evaluate the types of tasks and questions they present to students. If students begin to succeed when faced with complex questions and rigorous tasks, then instructional strategies and plans must be working. As a simple check, have someone monitor the questions you ask in a class period. How many of your questions have a simple, discrete answer? If the answer is above eighty-five percent, then you need to start asking questions differently. Try to pose questions that are debatable. Think about questions that people grapple with in real life. Consider the following examples that show how discrete questions can be refined to promote divergent thinking.

In a language arts lesson...
DISCRETE: What are the story elements in this story?
DIVERGENT: Why do writers break the rules sometimes?

In a social studies lesson...
DISCRETE: Why was the Civil War important?
DIVERGENT: Does war really resolve conflict? Why or why not?

In a science lesson . . .
DISCRETE: How does the water cycle work?
DIVERGENT: Is clean water a resource that should be shared across boundary lines?

In addition to different types of questions, different types of tasks are needed in all subject areas. Tasks should also provide students with real roles and real audiences. This means that the tasks should resemble real, adult work. They shouldn't be "teacherly" tasks that don't have relevance outside the school setting. Further, a good task will most likely incorporate several of the Common Core Standards for ELA at one time. This is critical because people often use several literacy skills in tandem. For example, I recently wrote a quarterly report for work about the success of a professional development initiative. In that report, I had to argue my point, cite relevant evidence, and employ appropriate grammar and mechanics. Merely practicing skills in isolation does not mirror the demands of college or career. Consider the following examples that show how tasks change when they employ real roles and real audiences.

In a language arts lesson . . .

TEACHERLY: Students will write a research report on an ocean animal.

AUTHENTIC: You work for the Endangered Species Program within
the U.S. Fish and Wildlife Service. The U.S. Fish and Wildlife
Service has decided to promote three endangered animals during its annual holiday fund drive. The departments serving the
selected endangered animals will receive a large research grant for
the following year. Create new marketing materials about your
endangered animal that will persuade your boss to select it for the
annual holiday fund drive. Your boss is looking for animals that
are unique, interesting, and appealing to holiday shoppers. Create a one-page informational flyer with images and facts. You will
present the flyer to your boss in a five-minute presentation.

In a social studies lesson . . .

TEACHERLY: Analyze the causes of the Revolutionary War in a three-
page essay.

AUTHENTIC: You are a member of the Sons of Liberty. Your goal is to
gather supporters for your cause. You must identify all the reasons
that going to war with England is absolutely necessary. Design a
campaign that includes leaflets, speeches, and other strategies to
spread your message. You must include your leaflets and speeches
in your plan. Your plan will be judged by John Gill, a leader of the
Sons of Liberty who works for the *Boston Gazette*. He will be considering the strength and clarity of the message as well as its feasibility.

In a science lesson . . .

TEACHERLY: Write a lab report.

AUTHENTIC: Design and test your own experiment. Present your
findings to a jury of your peers. Be prepared to defend your
results and share visuals that will help your audience understand
your point of view.

The instructional frameworks shared in the following chapters of this
book focus strongly on questioning that promotes divergent thinking and
authentic performance tasks relative to the Common Core Speaking and
Listening Standards.

The Standards Can Be Interpreted in Many Ways—How Do Teachers Know if a Task or Lesson Is Appropriate?

Yes, it's true. As a teacher, you can interpret the CCSS in many different ways. For example, consider the following standard:

ELA CCSS Writing Standard 2.B in Grade 7:
Develop the topic with relevant facts, definitions, concrete details, quotations, or other information and examples.

What exactly does this standard mean? Well, different people may teach to this standard by doing any or all of the following things:

1. Students use a highlighted passage provided by the teacher to select three quotations that develop their topic.
2. Students use a teacher-created electronic pathfinder to select from five websites to identify sources to develop their topic.
3. Students independently determine if they want print or multimedia resources, find them, evaluate them, and include them in their report as appropriate.

Clearly, each of the tasks listed is linked to the standard. However, which one truly *meets* the standard? Which task is rigorous enough to provide students with learning opportunities that will actually prepare students for college and broader life challenges?

Certainly you can reference the text and writing samples provided in the appendices of the Common Core Standards for ELA; this is a good starting point. However, other relevant resources that ensure tasks are on point are the *tests*!

Ugh, the tests. Yes, I brought them up in the second chapter of the book. Can you believe it? However, instead of viewing these assessments as the enemy, try to use them as a tool to calibrate the complexity of your classroom. They're coming, so teachers might as well use them to their advantage.

Now, let me be *very* clear. In no way am I suggesting that stale test prep is the best way to meet the demands of the CCSS. Instead, I am saying that these assessments provide us with an indicator regarding the types of questions that students must be able to answer. Also note that these questions should be a bare minimum in classrooms.

Right now, there are two organizations that are crafting annual, summative assessments for the CCSS: Smarter Balanced Assessment Consortium and the Partnership for Assessment of Readiness for College and Careers (PARCC).

The Smarter Balanced Assessment Consortium is developing a computer-adaptive test. This means that the questions delivered to students will be dependent upon their answers to previous questions on the assessment. If students are doing well, the level of difficulty will increase. If students are answering questions incorrectly, then easier questions will be provided. The Smarter Balanced assessments include selected response (multiple-choice), constructed response (essay), and technology-enhanced (drag-and-drop, select more than one, etc.) questions.

Alternatively, twenty-three states have joined PARCC, and this includes about 25 million public school children in grades K–12. The PARCC assessment draws from a collective bank of questions at each grade level. Unlike the Smarter Balanced assessment, students at a particular grade level get the same questions regardless of their performance on previous questions. However, there are three types of questions: evidence-based selected response (multiple choice), technology-enhanced constructed response (questions with more than one right answer), and prose constructed response (free response); this setup is very similar to the Smarter Balanced assessment.

Generally, both tests are much more difficult than existing state assessments. Given that some questions have multiple correct answers or free response, the days of guessing are gone! Further, the prose constructed response questions rely on several different texts, including primary sources and rich passages.

Let's return to the question and tasks mentioned above regarding ELA Writing CCSS Standard 2.B in grade 7. Figure 2.1 (page 16) shows a seventh-grade released task from the PARRC. Students must analyze the strength of the arguments within different texts. With this task in mind, only the final teacher-created task on p. 14 (Students independently determine if they want print or multimedia resources, find them, evaluate them, and include them in their report as appropriate.) for standard 2.B in grade 7 will foster the type of student outputs required for success. Students must create artifacts of synthesis and evaluation around complex, nonfiction texts without extensive support. This type of learning experience needs to be provided across many different content lenses, especially science and social studies.

Figure 2.1 Sample Seventh-Grade Task from PARRC

You have read three texts describing Amelia Earhart. All three include the claim that Earhart was a brave, courageous person. The three texts are:

- "Biography of Amelia Earhart"
- "Earhart's Final Resting Place Believed Found"
- "Amelia Earhart's Life and Disappearance"

Consider the argument each author uses to demonstrate Earhart's bravery.

Write an essay that analyses the strength of the arguments about Earhart's bravery in at least two of the texts. Remember to use textual evidence to support your ideas.

Given the rigor of these new assessments, many states are bracing for a dip in performance after the new tests arrive. The state of Kentucky, sometimes called the "guinea pig" of the CCSS, piloted the new standards and the new assessments in 2012. To help the public understand the changes, the education commissioner of Kentucky enlisted the Kentucky Chamber of Commerce to conduct a massive public relations campaign. The first administration of the tests revealed a twenty-eight percentage point drop in elementary reading. However, that was actually better than statistical predictions! Many experts believe that the trend seen in Kentucky will be experienced throughout much of the nation. However, this is not a cause for despair. Students can reach higher standards; teaching can reach new heights. It is simply imperative for educators to realize that "business as usual" must change. The frameworks shared in the chapters that follow share pathways toward the goals and outcomes teachers seek for their students.

In summary, the CCSS present all educators with an enormous opportunity to give their students a guaranteed and viable curriculum that will prepare them for college and career. While it's clear that everyone will be learning and growing together as these new requirements take effect, they will also offer teachers a substantive opportunity for national collaboration. Seize the promise and power of these standards, and use them to improve outcomes for all of your students!

Look Back and Step Forward

This chapter provided an overview of the CCSS in ELA, and you should now be familiar with the following concepts:

- ♦ The CCSS were written collaboratively by teachers, administrators, and experts from many different states.
- ♦ The CCSS raise the difficulty and complexity of learning at every grade to cultivate students who are college and career ready.
- ♦ The Common Core Standards for ELA have new instructional shifts that will affect classroom practice.
- ♦ The CCSS require close reading.
- ♦ Because many states have adopted the CCSS, a variety of resources are available from different states across the country that explicitly break down each standard.
- ♦ Complex questions and tasks are required by the CCSS.
- ♦ The Smarter Balanced Assessment Consortium and the Partnership for the Assessment of Readiness for College and Career are two different organizations drafting assessments of the CCSS.
- ♦ The rigor of the new standards and new assessments may cause a national dip in achievement data.

 ## A Question to Consider as You Reflect

How will the CCSS impact the classroom?

Now that you're confident with the demands of the Common Core Standards for ELA, you can consider some practical tips and ideas about successfully implementing the instructional frameworks contained in this text.

Bringing Curriculum to Life: Implementing Instructional Frameworks

Getting Started

The last chapter provided a general overview of the Common Core Standards for English and Language Arts. While the demands of the new standards hold great promise for students, to maximize the benefits for students, teachers must translate all the criteria to actual day-to-day instruction in the classroom. In essence, the goal of this chapter is to help you garner practical strategies and guidelines for using the instructional frameworks that follow in Chapters 4 through 9.

Importantly, there is no "right way" to use the instructional frameworks and ideas contained within this book. Try to open your mind and think critically when reading each framework. Your perspective, experiences, and ideas may help you bring a new twist, adaptation, or design to the framework. This is not only acceptable, it is encouraged!

Instructional Frameworks Are the Beginning, Not the End

The instructional frameworks for each Common Core Speaking and Listening Standard contained within this text serve as the seeds for good instruction. They are the beginning, not the end. Student outcomes are the end, of course!

As a teacher, an administrator, and a consultant, I've seen many beautifully written units that don't translate into innovative or effective instruction. They may look great on paper, but something gets lost in implementation. After much reflection, I've hypothesized that well-written units that flop in the classroom actually flop because the teacher is not open to the possibilities and opportunities that learners bring to the classroom themselves.

Brade Leithauser, in a recent *New Yorker* post, echoed my thoughts on this topic while discussing literature analysis. Essentially, Brad wrote about two different lenses that can be used to view a book: a keyhole and a box.

> Had I been still more articulate, I might have said that there's a special readerly pleasure in approaching a book as you would a box. In its self-containment lies its ferocious magic; you can see everything it holds, and yet its meagre, often hackneyed contents have a way of engineering fresh, refined, resourceful patterns. And Emily might have replied that she comes to a book as to a keyhole: you observe some of the characters' movements, you hear a little of their dialogue, but then they step outside your limited purview. They have a reality that outreaches the borders of the page (Leithauser, 2012, p. 1).

As soon as I considered Brad's metaphor, instructional frameworks popped into my head. (Yes, I really am that nerdy!) There are two different ways (described below and in Figure 3.1) to look at instructional frameworks, whether they are from this book, a state-level model curriculum document, or your teaching partner.

+ **Lens 1: Instructional Framework as a Box**
  If you think of an instructional framework as a box, then you think everything you need must be contained within the pages of the framework. You hesitate to venture beyond what is prescribed by the document, and you see the document as "limiting" to your professionalism. In many top-down educational organizations, this can be a common reaction or response. Viewing an instructional framework in this manner can hurt the educational experience for both you and your students. Viewing a framework as a box is often a way to deny responsibility for student learning. "I did what you said; I don't know why it didn't work!" might be your mantra if you see the world this way.
+ **Lens 2: Instructional Framework as a Keyhole**
  If you think of the instructional framework as a keyhole, then you most likely believe that the curriculum is a suggested series of activities and assessments that lead to desired student outcomes. As you peek through the keyhole, you can see all the possibilities that lie

Figure 3.1 If You Believe . . .

Instructional Frameworks Are Boxes	Instructional Frameworks Are Keyholes
The only goals that can be pursued are those prescribed by the framework. Assessments are time-consuming and take away from instructional time. Ownership over student learning is limited; you're just following orders. Instructional resources are limited by what is included in the framework or immediately available. Teaching is a lot of work.	Students guide the inquiry process and pursue their interests in light of goals prescribed by the framework. Assessments are rich tasks with which students learn as they create evidence of mastery. Control over student outcomes starts and ends with you, the teacher. Instructional resources are always evolving based on what students need. Students work hard in your class.

beyond the doorway. You can grow, extend, and adapt the learning in ways that will honor and preserve rigorous student outcomes.

As I am not one of those people who can see black and white without also seeing a million shades of gray, I'm sure that the range between "keyholes" and "boxes" is a continuum. Where do you fall right now? How can you push yourself to view these instructional frameworks and this entire book as a keyhole to improve your students' learning?

Most people who see instructional frameworks as boxes most likely will not experience as much success during implementation in their classrooms. As you progress through this book and through the year with your students, try to seize opportunities and extend learning as it unfolds.

Components of Each Instructional Design Framework

Instructional planning protocols can differ based on local preferences and school requirements, but this book seeks to provide you with all the tools you'll need to successfully complete virtually any planning template. Each instructional framework includes the following components:

♦ **Framework Goals**

This section provides you with broad, overarching goals for the lesson sequence. Such goals seek to answer the infamous student inquiry, "Why am I learning this anyway?" Sharing these goals with students and parents can help you provide a rationale for the learning at hand.

♦ **Tech Tools, Instructional Strategies, and Learning Activities**

This section provides you with specific learning activities and technology tools or instructional strategies that support them. This is where you can find step-by-step resources to bolster your day-to-day instruction as you work toward the framework goals.

♦ **Formative Assessment and Student Progress Tracking**

As you move through the learning activities, you need to track student progress relative to your overall framework goals. This section provides you with a sample chart to help you ensure that your students are progressing toward the instructional framework goals. Goals should be tracked and labeled relative to their learning stage. The three learning stages are acquisition, meaning making, and transfer. Acquisition is students' mastery of specific content. In short, they know facts or skills you taught them. Meaning making is students' making inferences about their readings, discussions, or experiences. This is where students synthesize main ideas, find common themes, and "read between the lines." Finally, transfer is students' taking what they have learned and applying it in unfamiliar contexts. Giving students many opportunities to transfer their learning will ensure they are able to use what they've been taught well beyond their K–12 educational experiences.

♦ **Final Assessment and Rubric Guidance**

Each instructional framework offers several different final assessments in an effort to reach all members of the K–12 continuum. Each final assessment seeks to provide you with irrefutable evidence that students have achieved the goals set forth when you began teaching the sequence of lessons. Further, students are provided with an authentic role and scenario, aiding student engagement. Rubric guidance is provided for the "capstone level" for all tasks. However, you'll most likely want to tailor these criteria to your specific students and your specific situation.

♦ **Suggestions for Differentiation**

Students are very different, and they may require specialized instruction. This section provides you with concrete ideas for providing students with multiple access points to the work without sacrificing rigor.

♦ **Window Into the Classroom**
Finally, the instructional design framework will end with the story of a teacher who has used the framework in the classroom. This will help you visualize how the framework might look in your classroom or content area.

♦ **Teacher Perspectives**
Teachers in different grade levels offer their experiences, successes, and failures when they implemented the framework in their classrooms.

Some Considerations About Instructional Frameworks in This Book

As the author of this book, I want to provide you with an easy-to-follow, practical guide to the integration of the Common Core Speaking and Listening Standards in all subject areas. Because these standards have been marginalized in state standard documents of yore, the need to highlight these standards intentionally is apparent. Students who can speak and listen with ease will do better in interviews, in the work world, and in personal relationships. However, you should consider a few things as you review each instructional framework.

Integrating Several Standards
Good instruction integrates several standards from both the CCSS for ELA and other subject areas. Although the instructional frameworks in this book highlight each Common Core Speaking and Listening Standard in isolation, you realistically can't teach one aspect of speaking and listening without considering and supporting the remaining facets of the task. For example, if you are teaching the ability to make a sound argumentative presentation, you must also teach delivery and cadence. To go even further, there are reading and writing standards implied when arguing a point succinctly during a formal or an informal conversation. Students need to read critically to ensure that they have the information required for success; you might encourage students to write various notes or drafts before their conversations. All the CCSS for ELA must be intricately combined through complex, meaningful tasks. The frameworks imply this type of integration while using a specific Speaking and Listening Standard as an inspiration.

Honestly, the selection of a single Common Core Speaking and Listening Standard is simply a coherent method of organizing and sharing different ideas throughout the entire body of the text. Be sure to consult the connections noted in the final assessment section of each framework for links to other standards from the Common Core Standards for ELA.

Technology as a Flexible Tool

Technology is a tool to help students understand the flexibility needed to seamlessly converse in today's digital environments. As you teach the Common Core Speaking and Listening Standards using the instructional frameworks contained within this book, the use of technology is emphasized. However, digital speaking and listening is only one (albeit important) facet of the competencies demanded within those standards. That is why there are both low-tech instructional strategies and high-tech tools for you to use in each framework. Don't feel pressured to use all the tools or strategies for a given framework; they are intended to provide you with choices and options, not shackles. Also, don't feel limited by the access to technology you may have in your current teaching situation. Speaking and listening can be authentic in many different modalities. One of the themes of this book is to stress the changing nature of speaking and listening given digital technologies while still honoring the power of traditional, face-to-face conversations. Be creative, get digital when you can, and make instructional choices that meet students where they are.

Technology Materials You May Need

All the technology tools presented in this book were free at the time of publication. To use them in your classroom, you'll just need the basics: a projector, a computer, an Internet connection, and a set of speakers. For some of the lessons and tools, you may want students to access them on individual computers, in a lab, or on mobile devices. These decisions are up to you and can be adjusted based on what you have available at your school.

Technology Is Not the Point

OK, one more important note about technology. Although technology is suggested and recommended in each framework, it is not *the point*. The identified goals, not the technology, should guide your instructional choices. If you think you could teach a lesson that honors the framework goals without technology, go for it. Honor the goals, not the tools.

The Role of Rubrics

A single rubric is provided for all the final assessments proposed in each framework. This is intentional. Each rubric is designed to show you the level of rigor demanded in every task, regardless of the specific challenge or format. The rubrics measure the competencies and goals demanded by the framework, not the task itself. (Consider this a reframing of the role of rubrics. Rubrics should be designed to measure complex outputs or competencies, not specific tasks. In theory, you should be able to use the same few rubrics all year in your class based on the competencies you are trying to nurture.) Also, the language used in the rubrics is to help you clearly describe the ultimate performance you desire from students. If you need to amend this language into kid-friendly terms, please do so. If you need to create "halfway there" or "getting there" categories for your rubric, please do so. These tools will help you provide meaningful feedback to your students. In some cases, you may even want to have students build the rubrics themselves with your guidance and the guidance of the rubric exemplar from the framework. One strategy is to provide students with the criteria and have them describe each word. This effectively creates a rubric for students to use that is accessible, relevant, and kid-friendly. If students can clearly articulate what desired performance looks like, sounds like, and smells like, their chances of success are much greater!

Final Assessments Mimic Real, Adult Work

Final assessments described in this book are intended to provide students with real, adult work. The goal of education is to equip students with skills they can use in real life; not to help them get good at "school." Such application to real life is often termed "educational transfer." To increase the amount of educational transfer required of students, try to minimize any prompting or help you provide students. The tasks should mimic the types of things people do every day at work and play. The assessments give students roles and tasks that are designed to engage them. To draw students into the relevance of each task even more, elicit outside experts to judge their work. In my experience, students become highly motivated when the audience for their work stretches far beyond that of the teacher. For example, I recently taught a unit on similar figures in math. For that unit, students had to design different video game cases, such as Xbox or PlayStation, for the same game. (The sizes of the different cases were actually similar figures.) As soon as I told students that someone I knew from the video game industry would be Skyping to review their presentations and designs, the tenor of the room changed. Students became excited, and final presentations became highly anticipated instead of highly dreaded!

Examples and Mental Models

Examples are very important as you start to consider ways that these ideas may apply in your classroom. Having a mental model of what you intend to try or implement can increase your confidence and success tremendously. That is why I included examples for every tool and strategy, a section that describes a teacher's classroom, as well as feedback from educators across the country. However, I realize that sometimes the gap between a "nice framework" and one that actually gets implemented is the *right example*. And alas, although I made a conscious effort to spread my examples across the K–12 continuum, every framework does not have an example at every grade level. (Every framework *does* have an example at elementary, middle, and high school levels.) At this point, I also think it is important to recognize that every tool or instructional strategy may not work at every grade level. You are the professional expert in this area. I encourage you to make adaptations and adjustments to meet your particular situation. I also encourage you to share your modifications at www.kristenswanson.org. Together we can build a community of learners and experimenters who seek to develop and refine ways to meet the demands of the Common Core Speaking and Listening Standards using digitally enhanced tools and strategies.

Day-to-Day Decision Making

When implementing an instructional framework, there are many decisions that must be made on a day-to-day basis. In which order should I present the activities? How long should I nurture a class discussion? Which supports should I provide students as they progress through the final assessments? This responsive, on-the-spot decision making makes teaching both an art and a science. I recently asked a large group of educators on Twitter to share the metacognitive questions they ask themselves when implementing an instructional framework to catapult their students' outcomes to new heights. Figures 3.2 through 3.4 are a few of my favorites from fantastic educators across the nation.

The question the teacher in Figure 3.2 poses causes you to consider existing misconceptions that students may have about the material. When students arrive in classrooms, they bring with them a wealth of experiences

Figure 3.2 What Metacognitive Questions Do You Ask When Implementing an Instructional Framework?

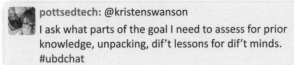

pottsedtech: @kristenswanson
I ask what parts of the goal I need to assess for prior knowledge, unpacking, dif't lessons for dif't minds. #ubdchat

and prior knowledge. However, all their presuppositions may not be accurate. To successfully achieve your goals, you must strategically debunk inaccurate knowledge that students may believe. It has been my experience that each body of content has a few common misconceptions associated with it. For example, students frequently believe the best way to argue a point is to list as many facts as possible. However, research has shown that a synthesis of facts and emotional stories will sway readers more quickly. Addressing these types of misconceptions at the outset of the framework will accelerate progress. Some strategies to ensure that you unearth and address students' misconceptions include the following:

♦ Do your homework. Know the most common misconceptions students bring into the classroom. Resources such as the Mosart Self-Service Site at www.cfa.harvard.edu/smgphp/mosart/ can help you learn about the most common misconceptions in science before you even meet your students.

♦ Develop pointed questions and activities that provide you with information early in the framework about what students know or believe. Instructional mainstays such as the K-W-L (what I already know—what I want to know—what I learned) chart can work, but also consider the power of providing students with a problem or scenario and observing as they solve it. (Early in the instructional sequence, it's their process, not the solution, that matters!) Seeing students grapple with an open-ended problem can help you not only figure out what strategies and knowledge they already have but also determine the exact content that students need to be successful later in the framework.

To me, the questions posed in Figure 3.3 (page 28) speak to the goals of the instructional framework. Do the goals make sense to you and your students? Can the students articulate the goals of the framework in their own language? Students must have a rationale for their work throughout

Figure 3.3 What Metacognitive Questions Do You Ask When Implementing an Instructional Framework?

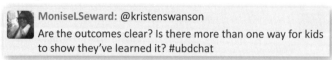

MoniseLSeward: @kristenswanson
Are the outcomes clear? Is there more than one way for kids to show they've learned it? #ubdchat

all stages of the process. Strategies to ensure that instructional outcomes are transparent to students include the following:

♦ Explicitly share the goals with students as you begin the instructional framework. Students can brainstorm what successful achievement of the goals might look like.

♦ Tell students a personal story about a time when you used the skills and competencies demanded by the instructional framework in real, everyday life. For example, you could tell students the following story regarding the instructional framework in Chapter 4: "People do this all the time. I recently hosted a virtual book club, and I used a VoiceThread to help people have meaningful conversations about the book I'd selected. The hardest part was asking the right questions!"

♦ Transparently track students' progress toward goals throughout the framework. After stating expectations clearly, give students progress checks toward the goal along the way. Your feedback will help them make changes that will improve their performance. Feedback can take the form of regular conferences with students (as is common in writing), checklists/rubrics (as is common in speaking and listening), or charts/reports (as is common in science and social studies). Be sure to check out the sample formative tracking sheets provided in every instructional framework in this book.

Figure 3.4 poses two questions about content/activity selection and the release of responsibility. Content/activity selection is still well within your control when using a framework. Importantly, you must select the topic students will explore as they practice demonstrating the skills and competencies demanded by both the instructional frameworks and the Common Core Speaking and Listening Standards. This topic or content area should be more than "just fun" or "fluffy." Though teachers want students to find school to be enjoyable and engaging, "random fun" shouldn't dilute their

Figure 3.4 What Metacognitive Questions Do You Ask When Implementing an Instructional Framework?

 jessicaraba: @kristenswanson
Some questions: Is this just for fun, or does it meet my goal? Have students had a chance to try on their own/when should I?

instructional goals. Content should be rigorous and relevant. Time is the most precious resource in a classroom; don't waste it! Strategies to ensure you're not spending time on things "just for fun" include these:

- Ask yourself: "What's the point of this content or activity in *real life*?" If you can clearly identify a link to what students will need to do *outside* school, then it's probably worth pursuing *inside* school. Once you've answered the question for yourself, ask a colleague, neighbor, or friend. (Preferably choose someone who does not teach what you teach to get a balanced perspective!) Can your colleague or friend identify the point easily? If so, you are on the right track!

- Have students reflect on how they may use the information and skills they have learned outside school after the framework is over. This can provide you with helpful information about the importance of various facets within the instructional framework.

Jessica's second question, the release of responsibility, is very important to successful classroom implementation. You need to consider when your students are ready to try different tasks *without your help*. You may recall that the term *educational transfer* was specifically referenced in Chapters 1 and 3 of this book. That term implies that students are completing a complex task without assistance from the teacher. To reach educational transfer, students need to work *on their own*. So how do you know when it's time to take off the training wheels? Strategies to scaffold to independence include the following:

- Follow the "I do, we do, you do" model. First, show students the expectation for skill proficiency, thinking aloud as you do. Then have students perform the skill along with you, guiding them throughout the process. Finally, have students do the skill alone, and provide them with timely feedback on their performance.

Vary the contexts as needed so that students become flexible in their thinking and performance.

♦ Ask students: "What would you need to do this on your own?" Make a list of the supports students feel are necessary to be successful. These might include working with a partner, using a computer to watch instructional videos, or having a small-group discussion about the topic. Provide students with access to these resources, and try your best to actively remove yourself from the process.

As you progress throughout the frameworks in this book, be as flexible as possible. Consider and reflect upon your choices each day!

Check and Adjust

In addition to day-to-day decision making, you also have periodic opportunities to check student progress and make major adjustments. Time in a classroom is very precious, and waiting until the end of a framework to consider overall success is pointless and wasteful. Formal assessments are not always needed to determine if a framework is "working." Instead, think of the check-and-adjust opportunities as routine checkpoints where you can evaluate the activities and materials you have selected.

W. Craig Fugate, administrator of the Federal Emergency Management Agency (FEMA), is renowned for his innovative and practical use of checkpoints in a variety of emergency situations. One strategy he uses often is termed the "Waffle House matrix." Waffle House restaurants are almost always open. If they close for some reason, they reopen as quickly as humanly possible. (Plus, you can spot the bright yellow glow of a Waffle House sign for miles.) So if a lot of Waffle Houses are without power in an emergency situation, then things are dire; help is needed quickly! However, if Waffle Houses are still serving waffles, a significant crisis hasn't been reached yet. When a tornado, flood, or hurricane strikes, Fugate asks all his regional supervisors to report the number of Waffle Houses that remain open in a given district (Steinhauer & Schmidt, 2012). Educators need "Waffle Houses." Teachers need quick visuals, ideas, and surveys that can tell them if they are in crisis (and need to redesign lessons and units stat!) or if they are not in crisis and should stay on the same path.

Here are a few "Waffle Houses" you can use as you progress throughout an instructional framework:

+ *Students do not persist on a task or series of activities.* This usually indicates that appropriate supports have not been provided, the level of rigor is not quite right, or the culture in the classroom is not safe enough for authentic problem solving.
+ *Students stop asking questions and only give answers.* If students have stopped asking good questions about what is being taught, then curiosity and interest has died. (It should also be noted that students should be asking vague and unclear questions—not only questions with "right" answers.)
+ *Students constantly ask about the grading procedures for an assignment or task.* (This is also known as the infamous question "How much is this worth?") If students are focused solely on extrinsic factors, then they may be compliant but not really engaged with the content. This warrants a major redesign.

Remember, the items listed above are "Waffle Houses." That means they are major indicators of a framework's overall design and progress. That's why they are all linked to student engagement and persistence. Because if students are not engaged, then the rest doesn't really matter. You can clear up misconceptions or revisit difficult topics. You can tweak lessons and graphic organizers and questions. However, once you've lost student interest and engagement, you must return to the drawing board.

Importantly, it's not always the flashy lessons that hold students' interest for an entire semester. It can be meaningful academic dialogue, rigorous content, and real-world tasks. Take Hapgood and Palinscar's research on science learning, for example. They noted that students are "eager to talk, read, and write about science topics. They love to compare their thinking with others' thinking—If we set the stage for it" (Hapgood & Palinscar, 2006, p. 56). Teachers can pass these checkpoints successfully and avoid closed "Waffle Houses" through the integration of both innovation and best practice.

Look Back and Step Forward

By the end of this chapter, you should feel confident with the following concepts:

♦ Day-to-day decision making affects the implementation of an instructional framework.

♦ Instructional frameworks can be viewed as "boxes" or "keyholes." View the instructional framework as a "keyhole," which opens up a world of possibilities!

♦ Each instructional framework in this book contains specific components to help you reach your goals.

♦ Asking simple reflective questions can help guide the day-to-day decision making that happens during the implementation of an instructional framework.

♦ "Waffle Houses" are the routine checkpoints that allow teachers to determine if they should significantly redesign frameworks or lessons. Most good "Waffle Houses" are related to student engagement because it is the underlying factor for all learning success.

 A Question to Consider as You Reflect

What are the critical steps required to implement a framework successfully?

You are now armed with a rationale for speaking and listening in all subject areas, an overview of the Common Core Standards for ELA, and the general principles of good framework implementation. In short, you are ready! Each of the following chapters provides you with an instructional framework that integrates subject-area content with digitally enhanced speaking and listening. Let the teaching and learning begin!

Courageous Conversations

Common Core Standard Speaking and Listening Anchor Standard 1:
Prepare for and participate effectively in a range of conversations and
collaborations with diverse partners, building on others' ideas and
expressing their own clearly and persuasively.

This Framework at a Glance

Framework Goals	• Converse with adults and peers in digital environments. • Monitor and synthesize themes and questions relative to conversations about challenging texts and topics. • Create and manage virtual spaces that produce asynchronous conversation.
Tech Tools, Instructional Strategies, and Learning Activities	• VoiceThread (tech tool) www.VoiceThread.com • Skype, Google Hangout, FaceTime (tech tool) www.skype.com, plus.google.com, or www.apple.com/ios/facetime/ • Today's Meet (tech tool) www.todaysmeet.com • Concept Attainment (instructional strategy)
Final Assessment Options	• Run an Online Bookstore Discussion • Make a Five-Minute Radio Segment • Prepare for a Chat with Grandma
Criteria for Success on Final Assessment Options	• Effective Digital Environment Design • Use of Textual/Factual Evidence • Use of Questioning • Active Listening Skills • Post-Discussion Synthesis

How Can This Standard Build Student Competency in Content Areas?

Conversation is central to all aspects of the human experience. Every content area can benefit from sustained physical and virtual conversations. Most workplaces require regular meetings or presentations that include familiar and unfamiliar colleagues. Many social rituals, such as weddings or religious events, often require participants to speak or present important ideas to one another.

Further, having intellectual dialogue about a body of content is one of the ways to inductively build personal expertise. As students take turns listening and responding to one another while citing textual evidence, they gain new insights about how to organize and assimilate new content into existing mental schemas. (That's a fancy way of saying that students can use discussion to make connections between new content and what they already know.)

Each content area relies on conversation to aid student meaning making. In math, students can debate mathematical proofs and discuss strategic problem solving as they encounter real-world dilemmas. In science, students can argue the moral implications of scientific advances or measurement errors. Social studies and history invite all sorts of debates and discussions about historical decisions and various treaties. In short, every subject can easily integrate this standard!

Good conversation is an element competent adults possess. Therefore, this standard easily supports education's ultimate goal: graduating competent adults.

How Does This Standard Develop Across the K–12 Continuum?

Most simply, this standard grows in sophistication relative to the topics and texts students should use as the basis for their conversations. For example, kindergarten students discuss kindergarten texts and topics, while high school seniors discuss twelfth-grade issues, events, and texts. By sixth grade, conversations should grow to include not only texts and topics but also controversial issues from the past and present.

The standard requires all students, K–12, to follow discussion protocols (taking turns, having roles, etc.) and to engage in multiple, peer-to-peer exchanges. As students mature, so do the structures of discussion. In kindergarten, students may use index cards with sentence starters. Sixth graders, conversely, should self-assign roles before starting discussions.

Regarding preparation for discussion, the expectation of the standard also grows in sophistication. By the time students reach third grade, they should adequately prepare for conversations through reading and reflection prior to the event. High school students should conduct research and systematic review prior to engaging in a formal discussion with their peers. Questioning during discussion is also an important element within the standard. For example, third graders are expected to ask self-monitoring questions of the group in an effort to enhance understanding. Twelfth graders use questions to hone definitions and issues while seeking a proactive plan of action. Consider Figure 4.1 (page 36).

In short, the areas of spiraling complexity within the standard are the following:

+ Topics and texts
+ Roles in the discussion
+ Amount of preparation
+ Use of questioning

About the Instructional Design Framework

This instructional design framework is titled "Courageous Conversations" and is intended to provide students of all ages with opportunities for sustained virtual conversations. This framework can take place within a single classroom, in an entire grade level, or across grade levels. It is meant to be very flexible and adaptable in response to the needs of individual students.

The activities and goals in this framework can be met with almost any content area. Specifically, content should be used as the *vehicle* to achieve the goals of this framework. Most commonly, this framework is used in conjunction with social studies or literature content. However, these commonalities should not be viewed as limitations. Be creative!

Framework Goals
+ Converse with adults and peers in digital environments.
+ Monitor and synthesize themes and questions relative to conversations about challenging texts and topics.
+ Create and manage virtual spaces that produce asynchronous conversation.

Figure 4.1 Context, Protocols, and Preparation for Collaborative Conversations

Students should be able to participate in a collaborative conversation given the following contexts, protocols, and preparation . . .

Grade	Context	Protocols Needed	Preparation Required
K	Peers and adults in small and large groups	• Follow agreed-upon rules, such as taking turns and listening	None
1	Peers and adults in small and large groups	• Follow agreed-upon rules, such as taking turns and listening • Build on others' ideas • Ask questions	None
2	Peers and adults in small and large groups	• Follow agreed-upon rules, such as taking turns and listening • Build on others' ideas • Ask for clarification and further explanation	None
3	Diverse partners and texts	• Follow agreed-upon rules, such as gaining the floor respectfully and listening with care • Ask questions to stay on topic • Explain one's own ideas relative to the discussion	Read required materials

Figure 4.1 Context, Protocols, and Preparation for Collaborative Conversations (continued)

Grade	Context	Protocols Needed	Preparation Required
4	Diverse partners and texts	• Follow agreed-upon rules, and carry out assigned roles • Pose and respond to specific questions • Review key ideas, and explain them	Read required materials
5	Diverse partners and texts	• Follow agreed-upon rules, and carry out assigned roles • Pose and respond to specific questions • Review key ideas, and explain them	Read required materials
6	Diverse partners, texts, and issues	• Follow rules for collegial discussions • Pose and respond to specific questions • Review key ideas, and explain them	Read or study material that is used to probe and reflect
7	Diverse partners, texts, and issues	• Follow rules for collegial discussions • Pose questions that elicit elaboration • Acknowledge new information, and modify personal views when appropriate	Read or research material that is used to probe and reflect
8	Diverse partners, texts, and issues	• Follow rules for collegial discussions • Pose questions that elicit elaboration • Acknowledge new information, and modify personal views when appropriate	Read or research material that is used to probe and reflect

Figure 4.1 Context, Protocols, and Preparation for Collaborative Conversations (continued)

Grade	Context	Protocols Needed	Preparation Required
9–10	Diverse partners, texts, and issues	• Work with peers to set rules for collegial discussions • Pose and respond to questions that relate to broader themes • Respond thoughtfully to diverse perspectives, and revise views when appropriate	Read or research material that is used to stimulate a thoughtful exchange of ideas
11–12	Diverse partners, texts, and issues	Work with peers to set rules for collegial discussions • Pose and respond to questions that relate to broader themes • Respond thoughtfully to diverse perspectives, and revise views when appropriate	Read or research material that is used to stimulate a thoughtful exchange of ideas

Tech Tools, Instructional Strategies, and Learning Activities

If you expect students to meet the rigorous learning goals outlined above, then you need to provide them with many scaffolded opportunities to engage in digital and face-to-face conversations. Given the availability of free communication tools on the Internet today, this is possible without expensive software. Four tech tools and one instructional strategy linked to this standard are listed below. Don't feel obligated to use all the tech tools or the instructional strategy shared here. Pick and choose the tools that work best based on your specific situation.

VoiceThread (tech tool)

VoiceThread is an asynchronous (occurring at different times) discussion board where students can leave comments as text, video, or audio. Because VoiceThread is asynchronous, students can take extra time to plan and reflect before posting a comment. This particular service serves as a great support to students who are not yet ready to handle the immediacy of fast-paced academic conversation.

The basic version of the service is free, and an educator version allows you to create log-ons for your students to use. In addition to being viewable through a web browser, VoiceThread is also available as iPhone and iPad apps. VoiceThread is a highly compatible tool, making it perfect to use as a bridge between school and home. To get started with VoiceThread, follow these three easy steps:

1. Go to www.voicethread.com and create an account.
2. Upload images or PowerPoint slides, or type text onto a few slides.
3. Share the slides with others, and encourage them to add comments!

I've seen many educators use VoiceThread in very creative ways to achieve Standard 1. Consider the following:

♦ A kindergarten teacher uses the tool to create a virtual journal between her students and their parents. Each Friday, students leave comments for their parents. Parents respond over the weekend, and many video comments are played in school on Monday morning. Sometimes, the teacher will leave video comments for students and their parents, creating a stronger bond between home and school.

♦ A third-grade teacher uses VoiceThread to provide students with discussion questions about their guided reading books. During guided reading, the teacher meets with several students in a small group, while other students read and respond to books independently. As they finish books, students go to computers at the back of the room and leave a video comment that serves as a "book talk." When other students in the class get stuck on what they should choose to read next, they can watch the video comments on the VoiceThread to hear peer recommendations.

♦ A middle school science teacher uses VoiceThread to have students orally explain and question what is happening in short video clips of experiments or real-life experiences. For example, the teacher uploaded a video of chlorine being dumped into a pool. Students had to comment on each phase of the process and ask critical questions relative to the safety and design of the process. Students were expected to use their knowledge of pH and water quality as they commented on the video and one another's ideas.

♦ A middle school math teacher uses VoiceThread to help students collaborate about strategic problem solving before they embark on a large problem. The night before they tackle the problem in class, the teacher uploads the problem to a VoiceThread. For homework, students comment on the problem with the following prompt in mind: What would you do first to solve this problem? Why? When students enter the classroom the next day, they divide up into collaborative teams to solve the problem. If they get stuck, they simply refer to their classmates' comments posted to the VoiceThread.

♦ A high school dance teacher explores different dance genres using VoiceThread. For example, when students get to disco, he tells them to find a piece of music from the era and capture a ten-second dance move from the era as a video comment. When reviewing the VoiceThreads, students are often heard praising and critiquing each other's "moves."

♦ A high school social studies teacher uses VoiceThread to create conversations among his students and the students in a partner class in Italy. Using VoiceThread, students debate current events that affect the students in both countries. Because the time zones are so different, the two classrooms would not be able to meet at the same time. VoiceThread allows both groups to leave comments at times that work for them, and it also encourages students to be reflective, active listeners relative to different cultures and perspectives. Without the digital tool, it is unlikely that such a rich exchange would be possible.

Skype, Google Hangout, FaceTime (tech tool)

Skype, Google Hangout, and FaceTime are all synchronous (simultaneous) video chat tools. Each tool requires a virtual meeting at the same time between two different groups or parties. These tools also require students to respond to the immediacy of typical, in-person conversations.

Skype is a free, web-based service that can be used on computers and cell phones. Students need a free account to use this service, and many teachers who use Skype in their classrooms have a classroom account for students to use. To get started with Skype, follow these three easy steps:

1. Go to www.skype.com or the app store on your phone and download Skype.
2. Create a free account.
3. Learn the account names of the people with whom you'd like to connect, and call them!

FaceTime is a tool very similar to Skype, but it is available for only Macintosh devices. If you are a Mac school, you may wish to explore this option for synchronous video chat.

Google Hangout requires a Google account. Google Hangout is different from Skype in that it allows multiple video chatters from multiple locations to talk to one another in a single Hangout.

1. Go to www.google.com and create a free account.
2. Put your friends in a circle on Google+.
3. Click the Hangout button!

I've seen many educators use Skype, FaceTime, or Google Hangout to achieve Standard 1. Consider the following:

♦ A kindergarten teacher uses a "Mystery Skype" with her students. Someone from another nearby town Skypes into the class. Students have to ask the guest questions until they can figure out where the guest is located. At the end, the guest reads a story to the students. The students like the activity so much that the teacher began doing it monthly!

♦ A third-grade teacher uses Skype to help students learn about the regions of the United States. She has created "Skype-pal" (like pen-pal) relationships with students in classrooms across the country. Students interview their peers in other regions to learn about different places in the United States.

♦ A sixth-grade teacher uses FaceTime to have experts share their science-related professions with the class each week. Students can ask questions and learn from people in the field while gaining exposure to prominent professions in the sciences.

♦ A ninth-grade teacher uses Google Hangout to provide homework help two nights per week for students. Students can log on to her Hangout and receive personalized assistance. One time when she wasn't feeling well, students logged on anyway and helped each other online!

Today's Meet (tech tool)

Today's Meet is a service that can be used either synchronously or asynchronously. It basically creates an instant chat room where students can leave text comments. The site has lots of features built in to enhance its relevance to the classroom environment. For example, students do not need log-ons, chat rooms can be deleted as soon as one hour after they have been created, and all comments can be exported easily to other file formats for later reference. Today's Meet is a great way to engage all students during a video, an on-site class discussion, or a mini-lecture. Conversely, it can also be used as a posting space for students to leave their comments at their leisure. Both formats work well with students.

1. Go to www.todaysmeet.com.
2. Enter the name of your room.
3. Share the link with your students, and get started!

I've seen many educators use Today's Meet to achieve Standard 1. Consider the following:

♦ A fourth-grade teacher shows her students a brief video clip, and they use Today's Meet to ask questions and note insights while watching.

♦ A tenth-grade teacher has students use Today's Meet to converse while watching the nightly news as a current events assignment.

♦ A second-grade teaching team has a Today's Meet page for each genre to be used during guided reading time. Students can leave comments about the books they're reading and interact with students in other classes.

Concept Attainment (instructional strategy)

Concept attainment is a strategy that was popularized by Joyce and Weil (1986). Essentially, this strategy guides students to use inquiry as they develop a complex concept. Typically, the teacher shares examples and non-examples with students. From there, students determine the criteria used to sort examples and non-examples, inductively building a robust mental model of the topic at hand. Relative to this instructional framework, students should use this strategy to develop a better understanding of what good conversation and exchange looks like, sounds like, and feels like. To implement this strategy, follow these seven steps:

1. Develop a list of examples of collaborative and non-collaborative conversations. The sample given in Figure 4.2 is just a starting point. For younger students, pictures can work well.
2. Have an open discussion with students: Why is each item in each group?
3. Label each list as "examples of collaborative conversation" and "examples of non-collaborative conversation."

Figure 4.2 Examples of Collaborative and Non-collaborative Conversation

List 1	List 2
Listens carefully	Hogs the floor and talks a lot
Speaks loudly enough to be heard	Speaks softly and looks at the floor
Uses full sentences and explains ideas clearly	Uses slang, informal words, and says "um"
Asks questions politely	Insists that he or she is always right

4. Provide students with additional examples, and have them categorize these items into the existing lists.
5. Ask students to generate additional items for each list.
6. Have students create an oral or a written summary of the concept of "collaborative conversation."

This strategy works well with students of all ages as you facilitate the understanding of effective conversation. (It works great with other concepts too!) To alter the level of rigor of the activity, simply adjust the examples you provide students. Consider the following examples for personalizing and using the strategy:

♦ A first-grade teacher works with her instructional aide to act out two different conversations: one effective conversation and one ineffective conversation. Students orally list the collaborative and non-collaborative examples used in the conversations. Then students practice the strategies in pairs.

♦ A fifth-grade teacher has two students converse and writes down all the behaviors they use. Then students sort the behaviors into examples of collaborative and non-collaborative conversation. Students leave the list posted in the room to guide them during their collaborative conversations throughout the year.

♦ An eleventh-grade teacher provides students with a series of quotes taken from a recent political debate. She asks students to categorize each quote into examples of collaborative and non-collaborative conversation. Students must provide justification for each placement.

Formative Assessment and Student Progress Tracking

Tracking student progress throughout this instructional framework should include evidence of student acquisition (relative to the content you've selected), student meaning making (via the scaffolded class discussions), and student transfer (when they complete the assessment tasks outlined below.) Both the Common Core Speaking and Listening Standard *and* relevant content standards should be included.

Tracking student progress along the way is significantly different from providing students with detailed rubric feedback on a final assessment.

The intention of collecting information about student progress is twofold. First, it allows you to adjust your lessons and learning activities to meet the needs of students. Second, it provides you with information that allows you to judge when students are adequately prepared to complete final assessments.

Explicitly teaching students about the learning stages of acquisition, meaning making, and transfer is critical. (You may wish to use more student-friendly terms with younger students. Consider *recipe*, *building blocks*, and *craft kit* for young students.) Be sure to share the learning stage with students as they tackle each task so they are aware of the cognitive demands and amount of support available. For example, one of my students once said, "I'm transferring, so I want to do this by myself. Can I check this resource instead of asking you?" Making students aware of the learning stage is a recommended best practice, and it gives helpful context to your feedback.

Consider the example shown in Figure 4.3 (page 46) from a chemistry unit. Note how the content standards for this particular example seem to focus on knowledge acquisition only. By adding the Common Core Speaking and Listening Standard, students gained many additional opportunities to move into higher levels of thinking, specifically meaning making (inferencing) and transfer.

Instructional Framework Final Assessment: Evidence of Goal Achievement

The role of a final assessment is to ensure that students have achieved the goals set forth by both the standards and the instructional framework. To this end, the final assessment options outlined here should provide you with irrefutable evidence that students can converse about academic topics and texts.

Choose texts and topics for each performance task that are grade-level appropriate, but the texts and topics must be novel for students. Practically, this means you should not teach the texts or topics you utilize during assessments. This ensures that students transfer their learning, which is of the utmost importance in rigorous educational environments.

Further, you will notice that a specific tech tool is not identified for each assessment. This is because the availability of technology is different in each school or classroom. Select a tech tool (the ones identified in the

Figure 4.3 Student Progress Tracking

Standard	Behavior(s)	Learning Stage	Evidence/Attempts Toward Mastery				Notes/Feedback
Common Core Standard Speaking and Listening Anchor Standard 1: Prepare for and participate effectively in a range of conversations and collaborations with diverse partners, building on others' ideas and expressing their own clearly and persuasively.	Use textual evidence during class discussions.	Acquisition					
	Use questioning during discussions to elicit broad themes from other members.	Meaning making or inferencing					
	Use active listening, and reference the words of others appropriately during class conversations.	Meaning making or inferencing					
	Generate new ideas based on conversations (reflection).	Transfer					

Figure 4.3 Student Progress Tracking (continued)

Standard	Behavior(s)	Learning Stage	Evidence/Attempts Toward Mastery				Notes/Feedback
NYSS Chemistry Performance Indicator 3.1 Explain the properties of materials in terms of the arrangement and properties of the atoms that compose them.	Know the definition of *atom, proton, neutron, electron, valence electron, isotope, atomic number, and atomic mass.*	Acquisition					
	Know different atomic models.	Acquisition					
	Know historical information about the evolution of the model of the atom.	Acquisition					
	Analyze atomic information to identify atomic numbers, isotopes, and elements.	Acquisition					

learning activities discussed earlier work very well) that best suits your students and your situation.

Final Assessment Option 1: Run an Online Bookstore Discussion

You work in a small online bookstore that serves a prestigious university. Each week, the bookstore holds a thirty-minute online conversation about a new bestseller as a way to increase book sales. This week, you are expected to facilitate the online conversation. Your job is to select a new nonfiction text, create an appropriate online space for the conversation, and serve as the discussion leader. Based on the conversation during the session, be prepared to share additional relevant texts that might interest the attendees via a marketing e-mail after the event.

Connections
Anchor Standards for Speaking and Listening: 2, 4
Anchor Standards for Reading: 1, 2, 10

Final Assessment Option 2: Make a Five-Minute Radio Segment

You work for a talk radio station near a large city. Each week, one of the most popular show segments is called "Courageous Conversations," in which a group of listeners comes to the radio station to discuss a current issue. Your job is to facilitate the discussion, record it, and edit it into a five-minute audio segment. It is critical that you highlight the most riveting and provocative comments within the time provided. After sharing the five-minute segment on the radio, be prepared to take callers' questions about the issue.

Connections
Anchor Standard for Speaking and Listening: 4
Anchor Standard for Reading: 1
Anchor Standard for Writing: 6

Final Assessment Option 3: Prepare for a Chat with Grandma

Your grandmother lives far away. Although you cannot visit each other often in person, your grandmother is a very proficient video chatter. Recently, you have both decided to turn your regular video chats into book talks. This month, she has selected the book. Make sure you prepare for the conversation by reading the entire book and thinking of several questions to ask your grandmother about the book. Then have the video chat with your grandmother.

Connections
Anchor Standard for Speaking and Listening: 6
Anchor Standard for Reading: 1

Final Assessment Rubric Guidance

You may wish to adapt the rubric criteria in Figure 4.4 (page 50) to fit the needs of your students and your situation. Only the highest level is provided in an effort to help you focus on the end goal as described by the standard.

Suggestions for Differentiation

Differentiation should always be focused on providing students with various access points, *not* altering the difficulty of tasks related to framework goals. (In short, don't water down the curriculum for students who struggle.) Instead, provide students with a variety of entry points to the conversation. Consider these four suggestions to enable all students to meet and exceed framework goals:

1. Provide nonfiction text passages in written, audio, and video formats to help students comprehend information prior to conversations.
2. Allow small groups of students to model good conversation while other students watch. Debrief the experience, especially the idea of active listening. Sometimes this is called the "fishbowl" approach.
3. Give students roles in the discussion. For example, a student who is not yet ready to ask questions may serve as a recorder until confidence is gained.
4. Ask students to design their own differentiation. Hold them to a high standard of rigor.

Window Into the Classroom

Jeanne, a high school science teacher, decided to integrate the ideas in this chapter with her unit on genetics. Last year, Jeanne noted that students were easily able to master the basic content in the unit of genetics, but they

Figure 4.4 Rubric Criteria

Rubric Indicator	A Description of Capstone Performance
Digital Environment Design	• Student creates an online environment that fits the needs of the audience. (For example, a backchannel should not be used with young students who can't type. Conversely, a video chat without an archive would not be appropriate for a conversation in a high school classroom.) • The online environment selected by students is easy for conversation participants to access and use. • Student provides a plan or instructions at the outset of the virtual meeting to ensure that technical glitches do not compromise the conversation.
Use of Textual/ Factual Evidence	• The discussion leader uses textual evidence to frame prompts and questions. • All members of the discussion refer to the text or factual evidence throughout the discussion to bolster and qualify opinions and viewpoints.
Use of Questioning	• All members of the discussion ask relevant questions based on the participation of other members.
Active Listening Skills	• Discussion members are polite to one another, even when expressing differing opinions. • Discussion members listen carefully to other participants and offer relevant follow-up comments and questions. • No single discussion member dominates the conversation. (The discussion leader should play an active role in preventing this from happening.)
Post-Discussion Synthesis	• Students synthesize discussion to develop new ideas and action plans. • Discussion members can articulate consensus decisions created during a discussion when appropriate.

had few opportunities to discuss the ethical implications of the tenacious topic. Because an understanding of both the process and the ethical implications were part of Jeanne's unit goals, revision was in order. To this end, Jeanne thoughtfully synthesized the following conversation opportunities from the unit materials in this chapter:

- ♦ **Learning Activity:** Students used VoiceThread at the beginning and end of the unit to have sustained dialogue about the ethical implications regarding genetics. This not only provided pre- and post-assessment data but also helped students crystallize their opinions on the subject. They left video comments for the following questions:
  - How far is "too far" in science?
  - Should we be allowed to clone people and animals?
  - Should people eat genetically engineered food?
- ♦ **Learning Activity:** Students conducted a Skype session with a local scientist who studies genetics. They set up the session, e-mailed the scientist the details, conducted an interview-style conversation, and synthesized overarching ideas in small teams after the session.
- ♦ **Final Assessment:** Jeanne elected to use Final Assessment Option 2. Students ran their own radio show, edited the audio, and placed the segments on the school website for teachers and peers to hear. Students used the microphones and recording software (Audacity, a free download, was the software) on the laptops available via a laptop cart. Students had to engage in thoughtful conversation on a targeted topic (about genetics), and then they needed to edit the conversation in a way that best communicated major themes and ideas.

After the unit was over, Jeanne was generally pleased with the outcomes students exhibited. Students were able to verbalize their opinions about genetic topics with much greater clarity and specificity than in years past. More important, students showed growing confidence in their ability to speak intellectually with both peers and experts. After analyzing student work products using the rubric provided in this unit, Jeanne noticed that the use of questioning was a weak area. She plans to integrate several mini-lessons into upcoming units to help students deploy this skill strategically. Overall, Jeanne felt the revised unit was a success.

Teacher Perspectives

For this instructional framework, three teachers across the United States adapted these ideas to their specific needs and situations. Read on to learn more about their experiences and successes.

> I had students use VoiceThread to discuss our study of local celebrations in social studies. The students liked using the tool, and it helped them be more thoughtful when listening and responding to their classmates. I ended the unit with the "call to Grandma" final assessment option. Students called a relative to plan a special celebration in their family. I was able to assess both their knowledge of celebrations as well as their speaking and listening skills, which are so important in kindergarten.
>
> —Katie, Kindergarten Teacher

> I used this instructional design framework to help me plan a unit on the 2012 election. Students used Today's Meet to run a backchannel discussion as they listened to several election debates. Then students completed graphic organizers and other tools to help them make meaning of what they learned. Finally, I ended the unit with a five-minute radio show. Students had to give their listeners an unbiased view of both candidates, and it was challenging! We posted our audio online, and many community members listened in.
>
> —Joan, High School English Teacher

> I teach sixth-grade physical science. When I taught my unit on different atomic models, I integrated this instructional design framework. Students were asked to consider this question: Is any model perfectly accurate? Students used Skype to communicate with a local scientist who helped them understand how he used models in his work. Students drafted questions and summarized the interview after the experience. Using their new knowledge, students ran a virtual conversation for the community on Google Hangout. It was motivating for the students to have an authentic role.
>
> —Jesse, Middle School Science Teacher

Look Back and Step Forward

Opportunities for courageous conversations occur in all phases of life. By giving students the opportunity to gain competency in this area *through different content areas*, everyone wins!

 ## A Question to Consider as You Reflect

Do your students hold better conversations in person or online? What evidence exists of this progress?

Bias Detectives

Common Core Standard Speaking and Listening Anchor Standard 2:
Integrate and evaluate information presented in diverse media and
formats, including visually, quantitatively, and orally.

This Framework at a Glance

Framework Goals	• Think critically about media in different formats (audio, video, graphics, oral) • Make informed decisions using media in different formats (audio, video, graphics, oral) • Detect bias in media (audio, video, graphics, oral)
Tech Tools, Instructional Strategies, and Learning Activities	• Wordle (tech tool) www.wordle.net/ • Gapminder (tech tool) www.gapminder.org • Mozilla Popcorn Maker (tech tool) https://popcorn.webmaker.org/ • Agreement Circles (instructional strategy) • Loaded Words (instructional strategy)
Final Assessment Options	• Create a Campaign Commercial • Record an Audio Website Introduction • Make Your Own "Pop Up Video"
Criteria for Success on Final Assessment Options	• Analysis of Bias • Effective Use of Bias • Design Choices

How Can This Standard Build Student Competency in Content Areas?

Information overload is a pressing problem in modern society. Some recent reports state that the entire body of information in the world doubles *every two years* (Mandell, 2011). Data comes in many formats: audio, video, text, and graphics. Each type of media has its own unique style for transmitting ideas, opinions, and stories. In short, there's a lot to learn out there!

However, drinking from the fire hose of information can be exhausting, even daunting. To make meaning of what is available, students need strategies. Essentially, students need internal filters that allow them to determine what is worthy of their attention.

Evaluating ideas that employ a variety of formats and perspectives is an excellent way for students to develop deep inferential thinking and information literacy. Dissecting a *potentially hidden* argument from a political speech or popular YouTube clip is something that will serve students not only in the workplace but also in life. Students must live as alert detectives to ensure that they can successfully navigate complex problems and issues. Further, sometimes the bias present in viral videos or infographics can be harder for students to detect when compared with traditional formats. This is because the information is often presented in an entertaining fashion that may skillfully put the content consumer at ease.

The ability to determine what matters, what is accurate, and what is credible is actually a bundle of skills possessed by competent adults. (These skills are commonly titled "information literacy.") Therefore, this standard easily supports education's ultimate goal: graduating competent adults.

How Does This Standard Develop Across the K–12 Continuum?

This standard grows in sophistication relative to how students respond to what they've seen or heard. In kindergarten, students must only ask and answer clarifying questions in response to auditory stories. However, by the time students are in fifth grade, they should be able to summarize what they've seen or heard with accuracy. The best way to consider the development of this standard across the K–12 continuum is to investigate the verbs utilized at each grade level. Consider Figure 5.1.

This standard requires all students to listen or observe carefully and respond thoughtfully to what they hear or see. As students mature, they

Figure 5.1 What Students Should Be Able to Do in Response to Information

In response to a visual, a quantitative, or an oral piece of information, students should be able to . . .		
Grade	Action	In Order To
K	Ask and answer	Confirm understanding
1	Ask and answer	Identify key details
2	Recount or describe	Identify key details
3	Determine main idea	Identify main point of story
4	Paraphrase	Identify main point of story
5	Summarize	Identify main point of story
6	Interpret	Evaluate how it supports an issue
7	Analyze main ideas and supporting details	Explain how it clarifies a topic
8	Analyze purpose and evaluate motives	Evaluate if a source is relevant
9–10	Integrate multiple sources and evaluate credibility	Create a new idea
11–12	Integrate multiple sources and evaluate credibility	Make informed decisions and solve problems

should begin to consider the credibility of the resource as well as what can be learned from it. By sixth grade, students are operating in the highest levels of cognition. (I would argue that students in younger grades are capable of beginning this type of evaluative work within familiar contexts. Be sure to check out the examples provided later in this chapter for more ideas.)

Most simply, this standard asks students to be careful detectives when they encounter all types of messages, especially oral messages. Since oral messages are delivered quickly and don't always leave a record, students must practice processing stories and facts to determine key takeaways.

This skill can be difficult even for most adults! In short, the areas of spiraling complexity within the standard are as follows:

- The level of cognition required after listening or seeing
- How the information is used to support future learning

About the Instructional Design Framework

This instructional design framework is titled "Bias Detectives" and is intended to provide students of all ages with opportunities to think critically about diverse media formats. This framework can take place in a self-contained classroom at the lower grades or in departmentalized classrooms at the middle and high school levels. It is applicable to almost any content area, as digital media relates to a myriad of topics and subjects.

As with all the frameworks in this book, content should be used as the vehicle through which you achieve your goals. Virtually any content area can be used to deepen student competency regarding the ability to respond thoughtfully to visual and auditory stimuli. Take a risk and try something out of your comfort zone!

Framework Goals
- Think critically about media in different formats (audio, video, graphics, oral)
- Make informed decisions using media in different formats (audio, video, graphics, oral)
- Detect bias in media (audio, video, graphics, oral)

Tech Tools, Instructional Strategies, and Learning Activities

To meet the framework goals outlined above, students must have ample invitations to engage with various forms of media. Three technology tools and two specific instructional strategies are shared to guide students on the path to competency for Standard 2. Remember to select the tools that best meet the needs of your situation and your students.

Wordle (tech tool)
Wordle is a popular word visualization tool. It is a free, web-based tool that is versatile and easy to use. To use the service, you simply type or paste a

text sample into the blank box. Within seconds, you will see beautiful word visualizations. Importantly, words that are repeated within the text sample appear larger in the visualization. This allows you to see themes and repeated ideas very easily. To get started with Wordle, follow these three easy steps:

1. Go to www.wordle.net.
2. Paste your text sample into the box.
3. Share your word visualization with the class.

I've seen educators use Wordle in very unique ways as they work within Standard 2. Consider the following:

♦ A kindergarten teacher uses Wordle to capture students' oral shares during the Star of the Week time. Specifically, students share their personal details while the other students listen for themes and big ideas. As the student shares, the teacher types the student's words into the Wordle box. When the student is finished, the teacher shows the word visualization as a prompt, and students recount the main ideas of the speech.

♦ A third-grade teacher uses Wordle to teach point of view and bias. She creates a Wordle from the traditional story of the *3 Little Pigs*, and she creates a Wordle from *The True Story of the Three Little Pigs*, by Jon Scieszka. After listening to both stories read aloud, students look at each Wordle and predict which story it belongs to. Students discuss how the point of view affects the words an author chooses, especially with regard to bias.

♦ A seventh-grade teacher uses Wordle to identify academic vocabulary in student textbooks. She simply uses the online version of the textbook to copy and paste chapters into Wordle. Then she uses the word visualization to select academic vocabulary words to preteach in class. Note: Academic vocabulary words, as defined by Anita Archer, are the words that litter nonfiction texts that *do not* relate specifically to the content at hand. *Equivalent*, for example, is an academic vocabulary word (Archer, 2011).

♦ A high school teacher obtains text versions of campaign speeches from which to create Wordles. Sharing the word visualizations after the class hears or sees a complex message can support students as they unpack main ideas and key details. A great site for finding text from presidential speeches is www.presidentialrhetoric.com/index.html.

Gapminder (tech tool)

Gapminder is a data visualization tool that can be used either online or off-line. It allows students and teachers to look at different data sets in real time. It uses sizes and motion to display trends across years, decades, and centuries. This tool provides a perfect primary source for media analysis in the classroom. To get started with Gapminder, follow these three easy steps:

1. Watch this video to see how Gapminder works: www.gapminder .org/videos/200-years-that-changed-the-world-bbc/
2. Go to www.gapminder.org/for-teachers/.
3. Use either the online or the off-line version to create data visualizations for your students.

Gapminder is an excellent tool for middle school and high school students to achieve the rigor demanded by Standard 2. Consider the following:

♦ A high school teacher from New York City's iSchool has created a research course inspired by Gapminder's tools. After modeling how the tool is used, the teacher encourages students to gather information about a self-selected research topic. Questions include such thought-provoking topics as this: How does the literate females-to-males ratio affect economic growth in China (Spevack, 2012)?

♦ A middle school teacher shows students a few variables graphed over time and asks them to create a story about what they see. Stories can be text-based or image-based, and many students opt to tell their stories through an integration of both text and visual ideas.

♦ An eighth-grade teacher gives students a deck of cards with country names on the cards. Students are directed to sort the country cards into any groups they deem appropriate. Initial reactions and groupings are shared. Then the teacher shares the Gapminder world map and asks students to identify different things they notice. Then students are asked to regroup their ideas. This supports the notion that there is a developmental continuum for countries, not just "rich and poor" countries (Geographical Association, 2009).

Mozilla Popcorn Maker (tech tool)

Mozilla Popcorn Maker is a tool that allows students and teachers to remix any video (even YouTube videos) in an online browser. You do not need to download anything to use this program. You can take any video and put captions, pop-ups, Twitter feeds, loops, and skips on top of it. It is very easy to use, with a drag-and-drop interface. Even young kids can use this tool. It is a quick, easy way to remix and annotate media. To get started with Mozilla Popcorn Maker, follow these six easy steps:

1. Go to https://popcorn.webmaker.org/.
2. Click on "Start a Project."
3. Paste a link from a YouTube video (or another video).
4. Click on "+ Events" on the right-hand panel.
5. Drag any remixes you need onto the video.
6. Click the "Share" button on the right-hand panel to share your remixed video.

Mozilla Popcorn Maker makes media remixing accessible to students of all ages. It is especially appropriate for teaching media remixing to young children. It's a great, interactive way to teach Standard 2. Consider the following:

♦ A kindergarten teacher shows students a clip from a popular educational cartoon posted to YouTube. Students ask questions about each part of the video. The teacher uses the "Popup" feature to overlay students' questions on the video. Students can watch the video and see their peers' questions as a center activity.

♦ Third-grade students watch popular commercials that have been posted to YouTube. The teacher guides students to use Mozilla Popcorn Maker to create remixed versions of a commercial with text overlays that describe what the director is trying to persuade viewers to do.

♦ A seventh-grade teacher has students find slanted news reports from various media outlets. Students then fact-check the report by adding tweets, popups, and text in Mozilla Popcorn Maker.

Agreement Circles (instructional strategy)

Agreement Circles can be used to encourage analysis and debate surrounding a piece of digital media or text. To implement this strategy, follow these seven steps:

1. First, have students read, watch, or listen to the content you have selected.
2. Have students create a large circle in the center of the room.

3. Ask probing, open-ended questions related to the content the students consumed. (You know your questions are good if students are truly split in their opinions!)
4. If students agree, they step into the circle. If they disagree, they stay where they are.
5. Students (now in two roughly concentric circles) must turn and face someone with the opposite perspective.
6. Students debate their points for a few minutes.
7. Students return to one circle and respond to a new question.

This strategy works well with students of all ages, even adults. It is an easy, low-prep strategy that encourages students to evaluate what they've read and share it with someone else. It assists meaning making for students, and it serves as a building block toward the transfer of knowledge and skills to new situations. Consider the following examples for using the strategy:

♦ A second-grade teacher reads students various selections from a Judy Moody story. Then she asks students to consider several questions about Judy's decisions. Students must decide if they agree or disagree based on their auditory comprehension of the story.

♦ A fourth-grade teacher shows students various commercials for familiar products. Students must decide if they agree or disagree with the benefits shared in the commercial. They use the words *biased* and *unbiased* to facilitate the analysis and discussions.

♦ An eleventh-grade social studies teacher shows students campaign commercials. Students must decide if they agree or disagree with the message contained within the commercial. Again, a specific eye for bias is maintained throughout the activity.

Loaded Words (instructional strategy)

Loaded Words is a strategy I used in my classrooms with both elementary and middle school students. It helps students analyze word choice for diverse media formats. To implement this strategy, follow these simple steps:

1. Have a brief conversation about the nature of loaded words. (Any word that is intended to evoke an emotional response is a loaded

word.) The teacher may need to model the identification of loaded words depending on the age and experience of the students. Showing examples and non-examples in a T-chart is one of the best ways to model loaded words.

2. Students consume a piece of content (text, video, audio, etc.).
3. Students create a list of loaded words.
4. Students work as a class to rank the loaded words from "lightest" to "heaviest."
5. Given the number of words identified, students reflect on the amount of bias in the media using individual written reflection.

This strategy works well with media formats that students can access repeatedly. For example, if you elect to show students a video clip, allow them to rewind and replay the clip when searching for their loaded words. This strategy also works very well as a guided reading station in the lower grades. Students can leave their loaded words in a pocket chart based on the story they're reading. The identification and ranking of each word supports meaning making for students as they grapple with complex, rigorous content. Consider the following ways teachers have used the strategy:

♦ A kindergarten teacher uses colored tape to have students high-light words in their guided reading texts that try to make them "feel something."

♦ A fifth-grade teacher has students find loaded words in their social studies textbook. After students rank the loaded words, she asks them this question: Is our textbook biased? How do you know?

♦ A seventh-grade teacher has students analyze primary source documents and videos (propaganda) from WWII. Students list and rank loaded words, and then they reflect on what they've discovered. Finally, students discuss the messages from WWII propaganda in relation to current media messages.

Formative Assessment and Student Progress Tracking

As students progress toward the goals of this instructional design framework, they should have the opportunity to receive feedback on all three learning stages: acquisition, meaning making, and transfer. Specific content standard indicators from your discipline should be integrated with the Common Core Speaking and Listening Standards.

Don't forget to share the learning stages of acquisition, meaning making, and transfer explicitly with students. This can be a helpful tool for them to use as they complete each task. Of course, feel free to modify the terms as needed to fit your students!

As shared in previous chapters, "along the way" information is much different from assessments that are provided at the end of learning. Tracking student progress helps you adjust your instruction, and it also helps students understand how they are doing.

Consider the example shown in Figure 5.2 from a fourth-grade social studies unit. Note how the content standards for this particular example seem to focus on knowledge acquisition only. By adding the Common Core Speaking and Listening Standard, students gain many additional opportunities to move into higher levels of thinking, specifically meaning making (inferencing) and transfer.

Instructional Framework Final Assessment: Evidence of Goal Achievement

The role of a final assessment is to ensure that students have achieved the goals set forth by both the standards and the instructional framework. To this end, the final assessment options outlined here should provide you with irrefutable evidence that students can evaluate and identify bias in diverse media formats.

Choose diverse media formats for each performance task that are grade-level appropriate, but the media must be novel for students. Practically, this means that you should not teach the media you utilize during assessments. This ensures that students transfer their learning, which is of the utmost importance in rigorous educational environments. If students have seen it before, it's *not* transfer!

Final Assessment Option 1: Create a Campaign Commercial

You work for the mayor of your town, and he is up for reelection this year. The mayor knows he will need to promote all the things he has done for the town to get reelected, specifically building a new park and opening a nuclear power plant. However, both these actions were somewhat controversial. The park took up land from a parking lot used by several business

Figure 5.2 Student Progress Tracking

Standard	Behavior(s)	Learning Stage	Evidence/Attempts Toward Mastery				Notes/Feedback
Common Core Standard Speaking and Listening Anchor Standard 2: Integrate and evaluate information presented in diverse media and formats, including visually, quantitatively, and orally.	Paraphrase main ideas from travel brochures and videos about each region of Ohio.	Meaning making or inferencing					
	Evaluate bias contained in travel materials about Ohio.	Meaning making or inferencing					
	Make decisions about current events after listening, watching, or reading brief news reports from CNN Student News.	Transfer					

Figure 5.2 Student Progress Tracking (continued)

Standard	Behavior(s)	Learning Stage	Evidence/Attempts Toward Mastery			Notes/Feedback
Ohio SS Standard 4.6 Regions can be determined using various criteria (e.g., landform, climate, population, cultural or economic).	Know the different regions of Ohio.	Acquisition				
	Know related vocabulary (landform, climate, population).	Acquisition				
	Create a map of Ohio regions.	Acquisition				
	Determine which regions of Ohio are most suitable for different occupations or activities.	Meaning making or inferencing				

owners, and the nuclear power plant has made many families in the town nervous. You need to create a thirty-second campaign commercial that provides unbiased information about the progress of the mayor's term while avoiding any words or phrases that could be offensive to community groups. Be prepared to defend the design choices you make in your video.

Note: You may want to alter the things the mayor has done to better align with your content area. In science, you could have the mayor alter the allocation of resources. In history, you could have the mayor close down a historical archive to save money for trash removal services. Be creative, and tailor the activity to fit your specific situation.

Connections
Anchor Standards for Speaking and Listening: 4, 5
Anchor Standard for Reading: 8
Anchor Standard for Writing: 6

Final Assessment Option 2: Record an Audio Website Introduction

You work for a website design company that is creating a website about (insert your content area here). You have been asked to create a compelling forty-five-second audio clip that will play when people visit the site home page. You must use loaded language to convince people of the validity and relevance of the content within the website. Be prepared to present your audio clip to the web designer and justify your choices.

Note: If you don't have the technology required to capture audio clips, students can perform their website audio introductions.

Connections
Anchor Standard for Speaking and Listening: 5
Anchor Standard for Reading: 1
Anchor Standard for Writing: 6

Final Assessment Option 3: Make Your Own "Pop Up Video"

You work for VHI, which wants to create a pilot for a new series of "Pop Up Videos." If you are not familiar with "Pop Up Videos," they are captions added to music videos that provide interesting commentary and fun facts about the musician or design of the video. However, VHI wants the new series of "Pop Up Videos" to debunk bias found in viral YouTube videos. Using the viral video (select videos in your content area) provided to you by the production manager, create a "Pop Up Video" that debunks any myths or biases in the video. Be prepared to share your design with the production manager.

Note: This assessment can be done with limited technology. If you don't have the time or tools to have students actually edit videos, just have them use construction paper to hold their comments in front of the video as it plays on a television or projector. I've tried this, and it's simple and effective at meeting the goals of the instructional framework!

Connections
Anchor Standard for Speaking and Listening: 5
Anchor Standard for Writing: 6

Final Assessment Rubric Guidance

You may wish to adapt the rubric criteria in Figure 5.3 to fit the needs of your students and your situation. Only the highest level is provided in an effort to help you focus on the end goal as described by the standard.

Suggestions for Differentiation

Differentiation should always be focused on providing students with various access points, *not* altering the difficulty of tasks related to framework goals. (In short, don't water down the curriculum for students who struggle.) Instead, provide students with a variety of entry points to the conversation. Consider the following four suggestions to enable all students to meet and exceed framework goals:

1. Provide digital media samples of differing complexity to meet students where they are.
2. Allow small groups of students to model their thinking for other students in the class. For example, have students report on their progress throughout the framework and how their thinking is changing. This will provide support to students who may not be able to see these connections independently.
3. Have students work in groups for the final assessment, and allow students to assume specialized roles. This can help students

Figure 5.3 Rubric Criteria

Rubric Indicator	A Description of Capstone Performance
Analysis of Bias	• Student identifies bias effectively within the digital media sources used to provide context and background knowledge for the task. • Student uses supplementary resources and facts to support his or her opinion about the digital media materials used.
Effective Use of Bias	• Student uses (or avoids) loaded language and ideas as necessary to complete the task effectively.
Design Choices	• Student is able to justify design choices used in the creation of the product. • Student is able to use data to support his or her design choices. • Student designs a final product that effectively communicates a message to a specific audience.

capitalize on their strengths as they transfer their learning to a new context.

4. Ask students to design their own differentiation. Hold them to a high standard of rigor.

Window Into the Classroom

Amy, a fourth-grade teacher, decided to integrate the ideas in this chapter with her social studies unit on regions in the state of Ohio. When Amy taught this topic to her students last year, she noticed that students were not able to clearly articulate why the information on regions was important. To increase the relevance of the content, Amy decided to use the topic to teach students to identify bias in nonfiction texts and media. Here's how Amy revised her instructional sequence:

♦ **Learning Activity:** Amy showed students several different travel brochures, travel videos, and selections from the textbook about each region of Ohio. Students used Agreement Circles to determine whether they agreed with each piece of media or text. Amy used the following questions to further deepen the activity:
  • Which region of Ohio is the best place to move?
  • How does where people live affect how they live?
  • Is everything that's nonfiction actually true?

♦ **Learning Activity:** Amy copied and pasted the chapter of the social studies textbook into Wordle. Students listened to a five-minute audio clip of the text and then paraphrased what they heard. Students used the Wordle visualization to metacognitively evaluate their paraphrased statements. This activity was repeated several times with key sections of the text. Following this activity, Amy led a group discussion on ways to listen carefully.

♦ **Learning Activity:** Amy set up region stations around the classroom. Each station focused on a different region of Ohio and used a different type of media (text, audio, video). Students went to each station and paraphrased what they learned.

♦ **Final Assessment:** Amy decided to select Final Assessment Option 2. She charged her students with creating a forty-five-second audio segment to analyze and entice readers to continue learning about the different regions of Ohio. Because she had limited access to audio recording technology, she used an old tape recorder to capture students' audio segments. After the assessment was over, students' recordings were put into a listening center that was used during guided reading time.

At the end of the learning experience, Amy felt the students had a much better understanding of why the regions of Ohio were important. Students were able to explain big ideas relative to tourism, manufacturing, and agriculture. Instead of seeing the regions as parts on a map, students started to see them as interrelated parts.

However, Amy felt the students still needed more practice with paraphrasing even after the unit was over. She decided to emphasize this in her literacy lesson to provide students with additional learning opportunities in this area. Overall, the revised unit helped students uncover big ideas about social studies content.

Teacher Perspectives

For this instructional framework, three teachers across the United States adapted these ideas to their specific needs and situations. Read on to learn more about their experiences and successes.

> I had students create their own "Pop Up Videos" using campaign commercials from the 2012 presidential election. Students had to fact-check each claim within the video and provide a "pop up" fact. Since we didn't have access to video editing software, students held up their cards as the video played. The students really enjoyed putting on the performance for their classmates. However, the most valuable part of the activity was the question and answer session that followed each "Pop Up Video." Students had to be poised and show true expertise. Students from other classes started asking if they could do "Pop Up Videos" too!
>
> —Carrie, Fifth Grade Teacher

> I started using the Agreement Circles instructional strategy with my class when we did current events several times last semester. To begin, students would read a provocative news article. (Many of the articles came from student suggestions earlier in the week.) Then students would determine their stance and enter the agreement circle formation. As you know, middle school students love to debate, but they often don't have facts to back up their position. During this activity, I could

circulate and prompt students to cite evidence during their discussions. Students had so much fun, they asked if we could try it in math to debate different solutions!

—Jim, Seventh Grade Inclusion Teacher

I taught the entire instructional framework to my students as we explored the topic of World War II. We talked specifically about bias, loaded words, and propaganda. The instructional strategies were really helpful. After students had many opportunities to read and discuss the content, I elected to use Final Assessment Option 1: Create a Campaign Commercial. However, I opted to change some aspects of the assignment. Students had to create a propaganda commercial to be played in movie theaters during the WWII era. Students could choose to create a U.S. or a German video. After students drafted their scripts, I had the digital media teacher work with them to film and edit the videos. Many of the students said it was the hardest and best activity they had done that year!

—Charlie, High School History Teacher

 ## Look Back and Step Forward

Being a bias detective is something everyone should strive for. Finding the hidden meanings in all different types of media formats is a life skill that can help students be wary information consumers.

 ## A Question to Consider as You Reflect

How does identifying bias make us better learners and citizens?

Do-It-Yourself TED Talks

Common Core Standard Speaking and Listening Anchor Standard 3:
Evaluate a speaker's point of view, reasoning,
and use of evidence or rhetoric.

This Framework at a Glance

Framework Goals	• Evaluate a speaker's point of view • Analyze the use of public speaking tools (claims, rhetoric, personal stories, etc.) • Detect bias from a speaker
Tech Tools, Instructional Strategies, and Learning Activities	• TED ED (tech tool) ed.ted.com • Edge (tech tool) www.edge.org • Authortube (tech tool) www.scholastic.com/teachers/lesson-plan/author-video-index • Somebody Wants But So (instructional strategy) • Semantic Feature Analysis (instructional strategy)
Final Assessment Options	• Plan a TEDx Conference • Choose the Best Sales Pitch • Plan a School Author Visit
Criteria for Success on Final Assessment Options	• Speaker Point of View • Speaker Components • Design Rationale

How Can This Standard Build Student Competency in Content Areas?

> *"It usually takes three weeks to prepare a good impromptu speech."*
> —*Mark Twain*

Watching a compelling speech can be as fast-paced and exciting as watching an action film filled with special effects. A good speaker uses storytelling to capture listeners' hearts and minds in a single swoop. In many ways, public speaking is an art form that requires charisma, wit, and impeccable delivery.

Central to a speaker's effectiveness is the ability to connect with the audience. Often, a speaker's point of view is a purposeful demonstration of his or her worldview, educational experiences, and personal goals. Effective speakers are like salesmen: they present their ideas in a way that makes the audience want to value and utilize their ideas.

However, there have been times in history when rulers and speakers have used their skills to lead people astray. Therefore, it's essential to separate the magic of a great speech from the actual facts. As consumers, students must ask these questions:

♦ What is the speaker's purpose for making this speech?
♦ What is the speaker's goal? Why?
♦ Do I truly understand the speaker's message? How do I know?

Students must learn how to synthesize and analyze the messages of powerful speakers for two primary reasons: (1) to begin to understand the qualities of effective public speaking and (2) to be able to use information presented by a speaker judiciously in an effort to enrich and inform their lives.

The ability to understand a speaker's point of view in both formal and informal settings is a critical skill for our service-based society. As digital networks effectively shrink the world, people need to be competent at managing interactions with others of diverse perspectives. Therefore, this standard easily supports education's ultimate goal: graduating competent adults.

How Does This Standard Develop Across the K–12 Continuum?

The core component of this standard is the role of the speaker. Students must be exposed to speakers who share information with varying levels of complexity. The rigor of this standard increases relative to how students are expected to use the information they've received from the speaker. For example, in kindergarten, students need to ask questions only following a speaker's presentation. By the time students get to middle school, they should be evaluating the credibility of a speaker's claims, including the identification of relevant and irrelevant information. By twelfth grade, students should be able to see the nuances that permeate a good speech: rhetoric, storytelling, personal stance, and emphasis. Consider Figure 6.1 (page 76).

This standard demands that students interact with public speakers. When first starting out, students are expected only to engage in a relevant conversation. As students mature, they should consider a speaker's words carefully, ensuring that the message is valuable, credible, and accurate. In short, the areas of spiraling complexity within the standard are these:

+ The grain size of analysis (statements, claims, an entire argument)
+ The level of cognition required to respond
+ The amount of critical assessment that occurs

About the Instructional Design Framework

This instructional design framework is titled "Do-It-Yourself TED Talks" and it is intended to provide students of all ages with opportunities to engage with prominent speakers within the local and global community. As a final assessment, it will also require students to plan for a realistic public speaking opportunity in a novel setting. This framework can take place at the classroom level or the school level. As each grade could process the appearance of a public speaker from the community differently, this framework is very versatile. It is also applicable to many different subject areas.

The topics you select should be used to help students practice and develop critical analysis skills while watching a speaker. As long as the content is relevant and applicable to students, then you are on the right track.

Framework Goals
+ Evaluate a speaker's point of view
+ Analyze the use of public speaking tools (claims, rhetoric, personal stories, etc.)
+ Detect bias from a speaker

Figure 6.1 What Students Should Be Able to Do in Response to a Speaker

In response to a speaker, students should be able to . . .		
Grade	Action	In Order To
K	Ask and answer	Clarify understanding
1	Ask and answer	Gain additional information
2	Ask and answer	Deepen understanding
3	Ask and answer	Offer related information
4	Identify reasons/evidence	Support an argument
5	Summarize	Explain how each claim supports a specific argument
6	Delineate claims	Identify which claims are backed by evidence and which are not
7	Delineate an entire argument	Evaluate reasoning and sufficiency of evidence
8	Delineate an entire argument	Evaluate reasoning and sufficiency of evidence while identifying irrelevant evidence
9–10	Evaluate a speaker's point of view, reasoning, and rhetoric	Identify fallacious reasoning and distorted evidence
11–12	Evaluate a speaker's point of view, reasoning, and rhetoric	Assess stance, premises, word choice, emphasis, and tone

Tech Tools, Instructional Strategies, and Learning Activities

Meeting this standard requires students to have a variety of opportunities to see speakers in person and via video clips. Speakers can consist of their peers, community members, and local business owners. Three technology tools and two instructional strategies are shared to help you create learning activities aligned to Standard 3.

TED ED (tech tool)

TED ED is the educational spin-off of the TED website. TED stands for technology, education, and design, and the site curates an amazing collection of brief talks from prominent speakers who perform at TED conferences all over the country. Speeches in the TED format are usually between thirteen and twenty minutes in length, making them the perfect instructional tool to use during a typical forty-five-minute block. Topics range from science to engineering to psychology, and the content sophistication varies as well. TED ED has selected topics most appropriate to K–12 education, and it provides teachers with a framework for customizing the student experience. Using the site, teachers can craft free response and constructed response questions to help students deepen their thinking and comprehension. Although I strongly believe these talks are most valuable when used as sparks for small-group and whole-group discussion inside your classroom, the question frameworks can certainly help organize student thinking before the interactive discussion takes place. To get started with TED ED, follow these four easy steps:

1. Go to ed.ted.com.
2. Click on "Register," and create a free account.
3. Browse for a video/speech, and tailor the questions and activities to meet the needs of your students.
4. Share the link with your students.

Because TED Ed is a relatively new tool, I've seen it used in only a few different settings. Here are some examples:

♦ A middle school teacher creates a series of speech analysis activities that students can do during their daily "team time." After a few weeks, the teacher hosts TED chats during which students can discuss the talks they watched and what they think about them. Students can enjoy hot chocolate to make the classroom setting seem like a coffee shop!

♦ A high school English teacher uses the "Playing with Language" series on the site to help students examine word choice and emotion within public speaking. Students each watch several videos from the collection and share findings with classmates.

♦ A high school chemistry teacher uses the "Making the Invisible Visible" series to begin the school year with his students. He uses this big idea (making the invisible visible) as a unifying strand through each investigation throughout the year. The speakers serve as anchor points for each discussion about chemistry, giving students appropriate context and relevance.

Edge (tech tool)

Edge is a community site that models itself on the Invisible College of the seventeenth century, which put some of the greatest minds together at a single roundtable. This online site houses many talks from an eclectic group of scientists, economists, and systems analysts. While the site is not designed specifically for educators, it includes orators who are engaging, quirky, and insightful. The talks are all different lengths, and you may need to show excerpts of talks to best meet the demands of your school day. These talks are most appropriate for high school students. To get started with Edge, follow these three easy steps:

1. Go to www.edge.org.
2. Click on "Videos" on the menu bar.
3. Use the topics on the left side of the page to find relevant speeches and talks.

Edge can be used for many different subject areas, but science teachers and social studies teachers seem to find the content most relevant. Here are some ways teachers have used the speeches at this site with their students:

♦ A high school social studies teacher shows students "Learning to Expect the Unexpected" at the beginning of the year. As students explore different topics in world history, he uses the speech as an anchor point. How could these people have *expected the unexpected* better in this situation?

♦ A high school science teacher allows students to select from several different videos from prominent scientists. Instead of focusing on the content of the video, students look for traits of successful scientists. They identify things such as risk taking, creativity, and play. This allows them to create examples and non-examples of scientific behavior during experiments and experiment design.

♦ A high school English teacher has students watch three different talks from the site for homework. Then students discuss which speaker is most effective based on the tactics used. This helps students identify different strategies and techniques they can use when crafting speeches or presentations.

Authortube (tech tool)

This tool is best for elementary students. Produced by Scholastic, the site is a collection of video interviews (or mini speeches) by authors of popular children's books. Students can read the texts and then listen to the authors discuss why and how they wrote the stories. To get started with Authortube, follow these three steps:

1. Go to www.scholastic.com/teachers/lesson-plan/author-video -index.
2. Look at the videos, and select a video-text pair that suits your students.
3. Share the video, and have students read the book.

Because many elementary teachers have access to texts from Scholastic, this is a popular site for many teachers. I found the following integration ideas to be particularly powerful:

♦ A fourth-grade teacher shows students the Dan Gutman video about his book *The Homework Machine* prior to reading the book. Students discuss the author's motivations and perspectives before, during, and after reading. Students begin to see how an author's life experiences can affect character motivations, settings, and plot structure.

♦ A third-grade teacher shows Andrew Clements's video before using *Frindle* as a shared reading. Students think about Andrew's experiences in school and search like detectives in the text for personal connections between the author's life and the text.

♦ A kindergarten teacher reads *Poor Puppy* by Nick Bruel to her students. Then she shows them the video in which Bruel describes how he wrote the book and drew the pictures. Using the speech as a basis for the conversation, students think about all the steps needed to write a really good book!

Somebody Wanted But So (instructional strategy)

Somebody Wanted But So is an instructional strategy I first encountered in Kylene Beers's book *When Kids Can't Read: What Teachers Can Do*. Although this strategy was originally intended as a comprehension strategy for fictional texts, it also perfectly lends itself to making sense of speeches. Try these four steps to use this strategy in your classroom:

1. Create a graphic organizer like the one shown in Figure 6.2.
2. Share the graphic organizer with students.
3. As students listen to a speech or presentation, have them keep notes in each pane of the graphic organizer.
4. Debrief as an entire class, identifying the worldview of the speaker, the author's purpose, and the resolution (if any).

Figure 6.3 is a completed example from Daniel Pink's RSA Animate Talk on motivation and his book *Drive*. You can view the entire talk here: www.youtube.com/watch?v=u6XAPnuFjJc.

This instructional strategy works well with all different types of students, and I've seen it used as an option for differentiation in some

Figure 6.2 Somebody Wanted But So Graphic Organizer

Somebody	Wanted	But	So

Figure 6.3 Somebody Wanted But So: *Drive*, by Daniel Pink

Somebody	Wanted	But	So
Daniel Pink • Author • Researcher • Storyteller	Bosses and leaders to use different strategies with their employees Bosses and leaders to stop using financial incentives in the workplace when creative work is required Bosses and leaders to use autonomy, mastery, and purpose as methods for organizing the workplace	Most bosses and companies are very entrenched in current extrinsic rewards systems that use money. The capitalistic system used in the United States seems to be in opposition to these ideas.	Bosses and leaders will need to take risks in the workplace to maximize motivation. To increase productivity on creative work, companies should provide space and freedom instead of extrinsic rewards. To increase productivity on creative work, companies should emphasize autonomy, mastery, and purpose.

classrooms. It simply helps students take notes in an organized way, and it also helps them focus on the storytelling aspects presented in many speeches. Here are some examples that show how some teachers have used this strategy to meet the rigor of Standard 3.

◆ A second-grade teacher has students use the graphic organizer to take notes when parents visit the school to talk about how they found their careers.

◆ A high school teacher uses the tool to have students analyze one argument at a school district board meeting. Students use several organizers to capture diverse viewpoints shared at the meeting around a hot topic affecting the high school.

◆ A sixth-grade teacher uses this tool to have students capture their learning during the annual eighth-grade science fair speeches. Students later share their notes with the speakers to receive feedback about the accuracy of their presented learning.

Semantic Feature Analysis (instructional strategy)

This strategy from Rachel Billmeyer's work helps students consider the effectiveness of different speakers using the following characteristics: rhetoric, personal stories, claims with evidence, and counterclaims (2010). (You can certainly adapt these characteristics to fit younger audiences. Consider categories such as personal stories, good facts, and exciting events.) The following three steps can be used to implement a Semantic Feature Analysis:

1. Create a graphic organizer like the one shown in Figure 6.4. (Remember you can change the categories at the top to better meet your needs. Even better, you can have the students brainstorm the categories.)

2. Students should put a plus sign in every box in which the concept exists, and students should put a minus sign in every box in which the concept does not exist. You can use this tool before, during, or after the speech occurs. If you use it before the speech, students predict what they believe will happen. If you use it during or after the speech, students use the tool to keep track of several different presentations.

3. When students have completed the graphic organizer and the speech is over, debrief the activity using whole-group or

Figure 6.4 Speaker Effectiveness

	Personal Stories	Rhetoric	Claims with Evidence	Counterclaims
Speaker 1				
Speaker 2				
Speaker 3				

small-group discussion. Ask students: What patterns did you notice? Why do you think that happened?

This strategy encourages students to compare and contrast several different speeches. It can be effective when students are considering several different examples or watching several different community members share their ideas. Consider the following examples:

♦ A first-grade teacher uses the strategy to help students keep track of the talk they receive from each shop owner during a town walk they take for social studies. She changes the categories to: "Tells good stories," "makes me excited," and "gives good facts." After the town walk, students compare their notes and share their ideas about what makes a good speech.

♦ A fifth-grade teacher uses the strategy to help her students enjoy the seventh-grade wax museum. During the wax museum activity, seventh-grade students dress up like historical people from the American Revolutionary period. They also provide very brief (one- to two-minute) presentations in character. Fifth-grade students must visit at least five different "wax sculptures" in the museum and record the speaking strategies each student uses.

♦ A high school teacher has students use the semantic feature analysis strategy to analyze and remember student government speeches. Students use this tool to analyze the different candidates and participate in a small-group debriefing session.

Formative Assessment and Student Progress Tracking

Students will need many opportunities to receive regular feedback about their performance as they prepare to complete the transfer task. You need to ensure that students move well beyond the acquisition level of learning. Meaning making and transfer must be emphasized and noted in your recordings of student progress.

Remember to share the cognitive demand and learning stage for each task with students (i.e., acquisition, meaning making, and transfer). This helps students to be reflective about the types of thinking and performance that are required for the task.

An integration of both Common Core standards and content standards can help you ensure you are meeting all expectations.

Consider the example shown in Figure 6.5 (page 86) from a sixth-grade math teacher. This math teacher draws from the Common Core Speaking and Listening Standards as well as the Common Core Math Standards.

Instructional Framework Final Assessment: Evidence of Goal Achievement

The role of a final assessment is to ensure that students have achieved the goals set forth by both the standards and the instructional framework. To this end, the final assessment options outlined here should provide you with irrefutable evidence that students can evaluate a speaker's point of view, reasoning, and use of evidence or rhetoric.

Create a learning experience for your students that utilizes the best speakers possible, both in person and via video. Community members, business owners, and other local people can certainly serve as resources. Because these people will be unfamiliar to students, the level of transfer required by the final performance task will increase.

Final Assessment Option 1: Plan a TEDx Conference

You are a TEDx local organizer. You need to find five people from the local or global community to speak on a topic or theme. (Feel free to customize the topic/theme to fit your content area.) Think big and try to find the best people for the role. Research local businesspeople and leading thinkers on the topic. Watching several TED talks on similar topics will most likely help you determine people to invite to your event. Your job will be to determine who the people are, schedule them for your event, and write an introduction for each speaker. Be prepared to defend your choices to the main donor for the event. Why did you choose each speaker? What do you hope that person will bring to the conference event based on his or her experiences and résumé?

Connections
Anchor Standard for Speaking and Listening: 2
Anchor Standards for Reading: 1, 8
Anchor Standard for Writing: 7

Figure 6.5 Student Progress Tracking

Standard	Behavior(s)	Learning Stage	Evidence/Attempts Toward Mastery			Notes/Feedback
Common Core Standard Speaking and Listening Anchor Standard 3: Evaluate a speaker's point of view, reasoning, and use of evidence or rhetoric.	Distinguish between claims that are supported by evidence and claims that are not supported by evidence in a speech.	Meaning making or inferencing				
	Summarize the speaker's main argument.	Meaning making or inferencing				

Figure 6.5 Student Progress Tracking (continued)

Standard	Behavior(s)	Learning Stage	Evidence/Attempts Toward Mastery				Notes/Feedback
CCMS 6.SP 1. Recognize a statistical question as one that anticipates variability.	Identify statistical questions.	Acquisition					
2. Understand that a set of data collected to answer a statistical question has a distribution that can be described by its center, spread, and overall shape.	Define a distribution using the terms *center, spread,* and *overall shape.*	Acquisition					
	Compare and contrast the answers to different statistical questions.	Meaning making or inferencing					
	Solve statistical problems from real life.	Transfer					

Final Assessment Option 2: Choose the Best Sales Pitch

You work for a Fortune 500 company, and several different companies will be pitching their services to you. (You can adjust the nature of the company and the desired service to fit your specific content area. For example, a pharmaceutical company looking for an experiment designer may work well within science classrooms.) You will need to create a rubric to assess each sales pitch. Be sure to include the items you feel are most critical to the success of the presentation. Are the facts/claims clear and accurate? Did the presenter relate the information to a personal story that made you feel at ease? You will need to submit your rubric for the presentations to your boss with a clear explanation related to its design.

> **Connections**
> Anchor Standard for Speaking and Listening: 6
> Anchor Standard for Writing: 8

Final Assessment Option 3: Plan a School Author Visit

You are the principal of your school, and you have received some money from the holiday fund-raiser. You want to use this money to invite an author to speak to all the students in the school. You need to decide which author you will invite and explain your choice. What do you want all the students in the school to learn from the author? Prepare at least three reasons for your selection to share with all the students in the school.

> **Connections**
> Anchor Standard for Speaking and Listening: 6

Final Assessment Rubric Guidance

You may wish to adapt the rubric criteria in Figure 6.6 to fit the needs of your students and your situation. Only the highest level is provided in an effort to help you focus on the end goal as described by the standard.

Suggestions for Differentiation

Differentiation should always be focused on providing students with various access points, *not* altering the difficulty of tasks related to framework

Figure 6.6 Rubric Criteria

Rubric Indicator	A Description of Capstone Performance
Speaker Point of View	• Student accurately identifies speaker's point of view. • Student effectively analyzes speaker's point of view for bias or slanted reporting.
Speaker Components	• Student identifies the use of rhetoric and effectively evaluates its purpose. • Student identifies the use of claims with evidence and effectively evaluates its purpose. • Student identifies the use of personal stories and effectively evaluates its purpose. • Student identifies the use of counterclaims and effectively evaluates its purpose.
Design Rationale	• Student is able to justify design choices used in the plan for the event. • Student is able to use data/evidence to support his or her design choices. • Student designs final plan that meets the needs of the intended audience.

goals. (In short, don't water down the curriculum for students who struggle.) Instead, provide students with a variety of entry points to the conversation. Consider the following four suggestions to enable all students to meet and exceed framework goals:

1. Use speeches/videos/topics that are at an appropriate level of complexity. Allow choice where appropriate.
2. Provide students with sample criteria for effective speeches, and have them apply those criteria instead of having them inductively generate those items.
3. Have students work with an older mentor for the final assessment. This can provide support and perspective.
4. Ask students to design their own differentiation. Hold them to a high standard of rigor.

Window Into the Classroom

John, a sixth-grade math teacher, always struggled when teaching probability. The students enjoyed the learning activities and chance experiments he shared with them, but he was concerned that students were missing the critical role that probability plays in everyday life. To increase students' ability to make real-world connections to the content, John decided to integrate a few TED ED talks with his curriculum. Here are the things John added to his instructional sequence:

♦ **Learning Activity:** John began his unit with a lesson he customized on TED ED. Students watched Peter Donnelly's talk on how statistics can fool juries. John added his own constructed response and open-ended questions that students completed after the video. Then John held a whole-group discussion on the use of math as a tool to make arguments.

♦ **Learning Activity:** John reminded students that probability is one of the most common ways speakers can make a point. However, many statistics can be misleading. Students watched a few clips from EDGE and completed a Semantic Feature Analysis. John added "use of statistics to inform" and "use of statistics to persuade" to the categories at the top of the organizer. From the activity, students generalized that many scientists, economists, and politicians use statistics to persuade.

♦ **Final Assessment:** John felt that Final Assessment Option 2 would allow him to effectively integrate the probability content he wanted students to master as well as the need to recognize the qualities of an effective presentation. He told students they were the heads of Comcast Cable Company, and the company needed to hire an outside firm to identify the segments of the population that were not taking advantage of high-speed Internet. This would help the company market more effectively. Students had to determine which statistics they would look for in an effective presentation as well as the other items that would ensure the success of the project. Students had to justify their plans in three-minute presentations to "the boss." (John invited the high school principal in his district to his class to listen to these presentations, and the students were both excited and nervous about this opportunity.)

At the end of the learning experience, John felt the students had a much clearer understanding of the ways probability and statistics permeated everyday life. Many students came up to him throughout the unit with magazine clippings or notices from television commercials that employed persuasive statistical tactics. Students were transferring their knowledge.

However, the addition of the new activities made John's unit run a little bit too long. He planned to eliminate one math activity and one speech activity next time to give his students a holistic experience while staying on track with the district's curricular expectations.

Teacher Perspectives

For this instructional framework, three teachers across the United States adapted these ideas to their specific needs and situations. Read on to learn more about their experiences and successes.

I used TED ED extensively in my class as an instructional strategy. However, students had to "flip" the lesson for other students to use. In essence, they had to pick the video that interested them, become an expert on it, create personalized questions or activities for the class, and facilitate the activity as students learned it.

There was a constant awareness of which speakers were effective as we showed each video. Also, students were amazed that I would allow them to choose any topic they wanted. It really helped capture their attention and engagement. Once I got out of their way, the learning really took off! At the end of the semester, students shared their learning via five-minute TED Talks. We hosted the TED Talks during the evening at our school, and we billed it as a "fancy event." It was great to see students sharing their passions with good evidence and poise.

—Anne, Eighth-Grade Teacher

Each year in our school, the Parent-Teacher Organization plans an author visit for all the elementary students. However, this year, I wanted students to help with the event. To start, we spent a lot of time talking about what makes an author great. This led to a great set of mini-lessons about what writers do to excite readers. We read a lot of books and reflected on strategies that authors tried. We also tried to apply those same principles to our writing during writing time. As a supplement, I showed several videos from Authortube, and we considered the speaker's point of view. We also considered how engaging they were as speakers. Would we want them to visit our school? Finally, I asked students to create a list of their favorite authors with specific evidence from their books. After sharing these lists, we worked with the Parent-Teacher Organization to make phone calls and organize the event. Students were so excited and proud when the day finally arrived!

—Teresa, Second-Grade Teacher

I'm not a traditional teacher, but I run the debate club at my local high school. I am always looking for new ways to have students analyze claims and identify a speaker's point of view. I started using Somebody Wanted But So during debate practice. This really helped students to follow the progression of the conversation and to proactively identify evidence to support their points.

—Jed, Debate Coach

Look Back and Step Forward

Being able to demystify the magic of an effective speaker is both empowering and enlightening. Once students can identify how humans communicate in formal settings, they can begin to engage in competent evaluation of these experiences!

 ## A Question to Consider as You Reflect

*How can students critically analyze what makes
speeches effective and compelling?*

Commanding the Boardroom

Common Core Standard Speaking and Listening Anchor Standard 4:
Present information, findings, and supporting evidence
such that listeners can follow the line of reasoning,
and the organization, development, and style are appropriate
to task, purpose, and audience.

This Framework at a Glance

Framework Goals	• Curate content and ideas that communicate a message clearly to an audience • Integrate multimedia effectively to communicate • Deliver information engagingly and effectively
Tech Tools, Instructional Strategies, and Learning Activities	• Prezi (tech tool) www.prezi.com • Glogster (tech tool) www.glogster.com • Storyboards (instructional strategy)
Final Assessment Options	• Boardroom Pitch • The Diagnosis • Pitching a Museum Exhibit • Goodnight Story
Criteria for Success on Final Assessment Options	• Empathy with Audience • Storytelling • Impact

How Can This Standard Build Student Competency in Content Areas?

As many parts of the world continue to shift to a knowledge-based economy, the need to communicate clearly has become an indispensable skill. Whether people are trying to close a sale, share an idea, or participate in a weekly church service, the need to present information has never been greater.

In today's world, digital media has allowed presentations to become interactive and multimedia laden. A good presenter is almost like a modern-day disc jockey who "spins up" a variety of images, sounds, and videos that emphasize and humanize his or her main ideas. It's not enough to read bullets from a PowerPoint anymore. That should not be tolerated in boardrooms *or* classrooms. Instead, students must use images, stories, and complex data to weave compelling narratives that engage and inspire audiences.

However, global connections and a seemingly endless supply of media make it even more difficult to capture an audience's attention. Therefore, it's essential for students to proactively plan a presentation that reflects the needs of the audience to ensure success. When presenting, students need to consider the following:

♦   What prior experiences may this audience bring to the presentation? How can I use those prior experiences to my advantage?
♦   How can I use stories to help my message "stick"?
♦   How should I use visual images and data to lend credibility to my work?

The ability to craft and share an important message is a competency all students should leave K–12 institutions equipped to perform. Being able to communicate and share complex ideas is something that is needed in all subject areas and all walks of life. Therefore, this standard easily supports education's ultimate goal: graduating competent adults.

How Does This Standard Develop Across the K–12 Continuum?

The core component of this standard is the formality of the presentation and the sophistication of the content being shared. Students in the elementary grades begin by simply describing familiar events, whereas students at the high school level are expected to present findings with a distinct perspective. The increase in rigor relates to the topic and the level of audience awareness. (I'm sure many of us can relate to a five-year-old who talks and talks and talks without regard to audience. Perhaps some of us also know seventh graders with that same problem.) Figure 7.1 (page 98) summarizes the nuances within Standard 4 as it develops over the K–12 continuum.

This standard demands that students share their knowledge through both stories and data. When first starting out, students should be encouraged to embrace their natural inclination to tell personal stories as well as stories they have read. As students mature, they should more formally present claims with evidence. By the time students leave school, they should be able to share a message keenly crafted to meet the needs of the audience. In short, the areas of spiraling complexity within the standard are these:

♦ The formality of the presentation (from telling to presenting)
♦ The content of the presentation (from personal experiences to facts and claims)
♦ The amount of customization for the audience

About the Instructional Design Framework

This instructional design framework is titled "Commanding the Boardroom" and is crafted with the knowledge that today's students will need to communicate ideas effectively in brief presentations with colleagues, customers, and friends. Today's modern culture embraces remixing and storytelling as methods for evoking emotion and communicating ideas. As a final assessment, students will be expected to deliver brief presentations that effectively communicate their messages to a specific audience. Especially at the high school level, students will be expected to mix different sources to create new ideas.

For this framework, the presence of a specific audience is very critical. For the final assessment to truly measure student competency within Standard 4, students must assume novel roles and create content for realistic audiences. This is what differentiates this framework from a typical classroom report. (Why do students really *do* those types of presentations anyway? To put the rest of the class to sleep?)

Figure 7.1 What Students Should Be Able to Do When Sharing Ideas

When sharing an idea, students should be able to . . .

Grade	Verb	What	Criteria
K	Describe	Familiar things	Providing additional detail with prompting
1	Describe	People, places, things, and events	Expressing ideas and feelings clearly
2	Tell or recount	Stories or experiences	Speaking audibly and in coherent sentences
3	Report, tell, or recount	Stories or experiences	Speaking clearly at an understandable pace
4	Report, tell, or recount	Stories or experiences	Using details to support main ideas or themes and speaking clearly at an understandable pace
5	Report or present	Topics, texts, or opinions	Using details and facts to support main ideas or themes and speaking clearly at an understandable pace
6	Present	Claims and findings	Sequencing ideas; accentuating themes; using appropriate eye contact, volume, and clear pronunciation

Figure 7.1 What Students Should Be Able to Do When Sharing Ideas (continued)

Grade	Verb	What	Criteria
7	Present	Claims and findings	Emphasizing salient points, using appropriate eye contact, volume, and clear pronunciation
8	Present	Claims and findings	Emphasizing salient points with sound valid reasoning and using appropriate eye contact, adequate volume, and clear pronunciation
9–10	Present	Information, findings, and supporting evidence	Paying attention to purpose, audience, and task
11–12	Present	Information, findings, and supporting evidence	Conveying a clear and distinct perspective while paying attention to purpose, audience, and style in both formal and informal tasks

Given that the premise is sharing information in an effective way, this framework can apply to virtually any subject area or topic. However, just make sure that students are presenting information about something that *matters* to them. As long as students are excited about the topic, role, and audience, you are on the right track!

Framework Goals

♦ Curate content and ideas that communicate a message clearly to an audience

♦ Integrate multimedia effectively to communicate

♦ Deliver information engagingly and effectively

Tech Tools, Instructional Strategies, and Learning Activities

This standard requires students to present information orally to a specific audience. Students should share their experiences and their learning in ways that invoke both emotional and analytical responses (the head and the heart). Two technology tools and one instructional strategy are shared to help you create learning activities aligned to Standard 4.

Prezi (tech tool)

Prezi is sometimes called the "zooming presentation editor." Instead of creating linear PowerPoint or slide presentations, Prezi allows students to create nonlinear multimedia supports to accompany a presentation. Students can add video, images, and text to either a free-form or a designed path that supports their presentations or verbal reports. The site is best used as a creation tool. The tool can be used with varying levels of sophistication, and I have found it most suitable with students in grades 3–12. To get started with Prezi, follow these three easy steps:

1. Go to edu.prezi.com/.
2. Click on "Sign Up Now" on the top right of the screen, and create a free account.
3. Add video, images, and a path for your media that complements your speaking points.

Prezi has been used extensively in K–12 and universities. There is even a library of templates, sites, and tips that teachers can use. The vibrant community includes many integration areas. Specifically, I noticed the following:

♦ A teacher who wants his students to understand note taking as "literacy" shares this presentation with his students and other teachers at his school. See it here: prezi.com/nvlfkoeuxtl-/active-reading-and-note-taking-with-or-without-technology/.

♦ A middle school is using Prezi when students make presentations throughout their social studies units. See one student example here: prezi.com/ytj-dox2gmk5/bill-of-rights-for-dummies/.

♦ A middle school teacher has students share information about one piece of art from the Renaissance. See an example here: prezi.com/bcjotaqhdpdv/copy-of-agony-in-the-garden-giovanni-bellini/.

♦ A psychology teacher has his students share information about a psychological disorder. He specifically asks students to use images more than text, helping them focus on the supplementary role that multimedia plays during a verbal presentation. See an example here: prezi.com/phnmlaicxygz/ergophobia-2/.

♦ A fourth-grade teacher has her students use Prezi to create collaborative timelines about the history of North Carolina. Students engage in a lot of thinking and meaning making before they actually record their learning with Prezi. See an example here: http://prezi.com/0nth-erdzi2s/history-of-north-carolina/.

Glogster (tech tool)

Glogster creates digital posters that can include audio, video, images, and text. Think of it as nonlinear way to organize assets that your students will need to share during a presentation. In some ways, it can help your students see the connections between topics, and it can be a canvas for them to organize their ideas. To get started with Glogster, follow these three easy steps:

1. Go to edu.glogster.com/.
2. Click on "For Your Classroom."
3. Create your teacher profile, and distribute user names to your students.

Glogster works well with many different subject areas as well as different ages of students. Consider the following examples:

Figure 7.2 Stonyboard Grid

♦ An elementary teacher has students create Glogs about their favorite books before they give "book chats." This helps students organize their thoughts prior to the talks, gives a helpful visual during the book chats, and generates a library of artifacts for students to browse when they need a book recommendation.

♦ A high school librarian has students share their research findings for a culminating project using Glogster. This helps students make their research "digestible" to the greater public during their presentations as compared to traditional five-page reports.

Storyboards (instructional strategy)

Using storyboards is an instructional strategy in which students draw small frames that explain the key points of their speeches or presentations as narratives. This helps students visualize the "plot" of their presentations and the ways the concepts relate to one another. For example, an upper elementary presentation on economics could include characters such as "supply" and "demand" that must find balance as a resolution. Further, outlining the ideas of a verbal presentation and creating a story from the content (complete with personal stories) encourages students to create compelling speeches that leave emotional impressions on the audience. Try these four steps to use this strategy in your classroom:

1. Provide students with a large paper with boxes (Figure 7.2). You can adjust the number of boxes to fit the complexity of the task.
2. Have students sketch or draw each segment of their speeches. This may take several revisions, and pencils are recommended!
3. Have students write captions for each image.
4. Have students use the captions and images to draft, practice, and present their ideas.

Figure 7.3 (page 104) shows a storyboard from a second grader for his short talk on the water cycle.

Teachers commonly use this strategy with elementary students to help them draft stories, but it can help students of all ages draft speeches or presentations. Here are some ways teachers use this strategy to support their students as they seek to meet the demands of Standard 4.

♦ A first-grade teacher provides students with three storyboard frames: beginning, middle, and end. Students sketch the main idea

Figure 7.3 Water Cycle Storyboard

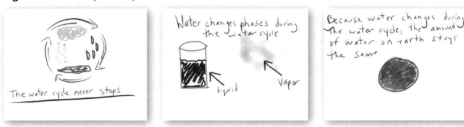

for each part of their speeches about insects. Students share their presentations with the class, and they use their storyboards to cue them as they share.

♦ A middle school teacher has students storyboard presentations in which they assume the role of characters in *Anne Frank: The Diary of a Young Girl*. Students use the storyboards to select the relevant details they will include and how they will thoughtfully capture the perspective of the characters they've selected.

♦ A high school teacher uses storyboards to help students organize their points in a debate. Students have to craft a compelling narrative that will help convince people who may be undecided on the issue. Students use the storyboard strategy to ensure they have stories people will remember about their topics.

Formative Assessment and Student Progress Tracking

Delivering a speech or presentation effectively relies on an innumerable number of interrelated variables. Students will need timely, specific feedback so they improve over time. Sometimes, due to the time required to watch speeches, giving students feedback "along the way" can be difficult. To this end, help students identify strengths and weaknesses in their own work and the work of their peers. This multiplies the opportunities students have to garner information about their performance.

Because it is impossible to think about meaningful presentations without meaningful content, an integration of both Common Core standards and subject area standards will be required. Also, remember to share the learning stage with students for each task. This will help them employ appropriate metacogntive strategies as they grapple with each challenge.

Consider the example shown in Figure 7.4 from a second-grade social studies teacher. The teacher has students retell stories from history using

Figure 7.4 Student Progress Tracking

Standard	Behavior(s)	Learning Stage	Evidence/Attempts Towards Mastery				Notes/Feedback
Common Core Standard Speaking and Listening Anchor Standard 4: Present information, findings, and supporting evidence such that listeners can follow the line of reasoning, and the organization, development, and style are appropriate to task, purpose, and audience.	Tell a story (from history) with relevant details that are in order.	Transfer					
	Use appropriate volume, and complete sentences when sharing a story orally.	Transfer					
PA His. 8.1.2 A 1. Read and interpret information on simple time lines.	Read the dates on a timeline.	Acquisition					
	Determine which dates are most important to retell.	Meaning making or inferencing					

timelines as guides. This teacher draws from the Common Core Speaking and Listening Standards as well as the Pennsylvania History standards.

Instructional Framework Final Assessment: Evidence of Goal Achievement

The final assessment of this instructional framework requires students to deliver presentations in situations that are novel or unfamiliar. Students must master content on their own and share it effectively. Unless students can create and share engaging presentations without the direct assistance of the teacher, then the rigor of the standard has not been preserved. To this end, the final assessment options outlined here should provide students with a specific role, audience, and content area. This will allow students to practice the work that adults do every day.

Final Assessment Option 1: Boardroom Pitch

You are the head of a small, start-up company. Your company is trying to gain investors for your new product or service. (Try to choose a product or service that is well suited to your content area. For example, a biology teacher may choose innovative pharmaceutical products, or a history teacher may choose a digital archive of Native American artifacts.)You have five minutes to convince investors that your product or service is viable and worthy of a significant investment. Use visuals or graphs to support your points. Be prepared to answer questions from your investors after your pitch.

> **Connections**
> Anchor Standard for Speaking and Listening: 5
> Anchor Standard for Reading: 1

Final Assessment Option 2: The Diagnosis

You are a doctor (Try to choose a role that fits your content area: psychologist, medical doctor, etc.), and a patient has entered your office. You must try to solve the patient's problems and present an official diagnosis. (Science teachers could have students diagnose a patient with a specific illness or chemical exposure. Literature teachers could have students diagnose a character from a piece of literature, such as Jay Gatsby from *The Great Gatsby*.) The official diagnosis you share with your patient should appeal to the patient's specific personality, interests, and problems. Visuals may be needed to help you make your point more clearly. Be prepared to answer any questions your patient may have.

Connections
Anchor Standards for Speaking and Listening: 1, 5
Anchor Standard for Reading: 1

Final Assessment Option 3: Pitching a Museum Exhibit

You are the curator of a museum, and you must persuade the board of directors to open a new museum exhibit. (The topic of this exhibit should be closely related to the relevant content area. Allowing student choice from a range of topics is also recommended.) You should provide images and/or sketches of what the exhibit might look like, why the exhibit is important, and who is most likely to enjoy the exhibit.

Connections
Anchor Standards for Speaking and Listening: 5, 6
Anchor Standard for Reading: 1

Final Assessment Option 4: Goodnight Story

This assessment option is specifically designed for students in the early elementary grades. A careful review of the standards reveals that students in the early elementary grades are required to tell stories from either their own experience or a familiar text. This task is designed to specifically meet those needs.

You are having three friends over to your house for a sleepover. Before you go to bed, you want to tell your friends a "goodnight story." Make sure you include all the important details from the story in order. The story can be one you make up, or it can be one you've read. When you are finished, be sure to ask your friends if they have any questions!

Connections
Anchor Standard for Speaking and Listening: 1
Anchor Standard for Reading: 3

Final Assessment Rubric Guidance

You may wish to adapt the rubric criteria in Figure 7.5 to fit the needs of your students and your situation. Only the highest level is provided in an effort to help you focus on the end goal as described by the standard.

Suggestions for Differentiation

Differentiation can help students access the standards from a variety of access points; however, the rigor of each standard should not be sacrificed. All students, regardless of their levels of readiness or interest, should practice sharing content with others in formal and informal presentations. Consider the following four suggestions to assist diverse learners as they complete the instructional design framework offered in this chapter:

1. Allow some students to video record parts of their presentations to reduce the amount of "on-demand" time required during a presentation.
2. Use content area topics that are at an appropriate level of complexity. When learning the content for their presentations, provide topic and format diversity (i.e., provide students with videos, text, and images to learn about the content).
3. Have students complete their presentations in small groups or with partners.
4. Ask students to design their own differentiation. Hold them to a high standard of rigor.

Window Into the Classroom

Carrie, a first-grade teacher, wanted to give her students opportunities to formally present their learning to older students. Although the students frequently presented what they had read to their peers, they did not share this learning with other students in the school. Carrie used the instructional design framework in this chapter to help her students make relationships about reading with older students who could serve as mentors and motivators. This was all done while affording young students many

Figure 7.5 Rubric Criteria

Rubric Indicator	A Description of Capstone Performance
Empathy with Audience	• The presentation effectively targets the needs of the audience with regard to word choice, topic selection, and details/facts. • The speaker is viewed as credible by the audience due to specific actions taken by the speaker at the beginning of the talk (use of engaging introduction, relevant personal details, clear facts, etc.).
Storytelling	• The presentation creates a compelling narrative, regardless of the topic. • The presentation is easy to remember and understand because each element is interconnected. • The speaker uses several (personal or otherwise) stories to help the audience create connections to the content.
Impact	• The presentation effectively garners an emotional response from the audience. • The presentation uses facts in a way that elicits a response from the audience. • The presentation uses visuals in a way that elicits a response from the audience.

opportunities to present their learning. Here are the things Carrie used in her classroom:

1. **Learning Activity:** Carrie began her unit with a lesson based upon Leo Lionni's book *Swimmy.* She read the book to students and created a nonlinear Prezi with pictures from the book. The Prezi was projected onto a whiteboard, and Carrie modeled retelling the book while clicking on images that supported her point. Students practiced pair reading (or listening) and retelling using the Prezi for a week during center time.

2. **Learning Activity:** Students read books at their appropriate reading level. They each selected a book (a favorite) to share with a peer in the class. Students used the storyboard technique to draw out the key elements of the stories they wanted to share. Students used the storyboard pictures as they retold their stories to peers. This was practiced with different texts for about a month.

3. **Final Assessment:** Carrie decided to use Final Assessment Option 4 because she wanted her students to focus on retelling a text. Carrie told students that fourth graders would be visiting to learn more about the books the first graders were reading. When the fourth-grade students arrived, each of Carrie's first graders selected a familiar book from the book basket and shared what the book was about and why he or she liked it. During this time, students could use their storyboards if they felt they needed to. (Carrie encouraged them to do the task without the storyboards, but they provided differentiated aid to those who needed it.) Carrie and her fourth-grade teaching partner circulated the room to score students using rubrics adapted from the final assessment rubric provided in this chapter.

At the end of the learning experience, Carrie felt her students had been offered many new opportunities to share and present their readings to students of different ages. She saw the first graders gaining confidence in both their reading and verbal sharing skills through increased practice and direct instruction with storyboards.

However, Carrie wanted to continue to give her students practice in this area. So after the unit was over, she created ten more nonlinear Prezi presentations based on the class's favorite books and had students retell these stories during center time. This helped students continue to use the skill in new contexts well beyond the scope of the individual unit.

Teacher Perspectives

For this instructional framework, two teachers across the United States adapted these ideas to their specific needs and situations. Read on to learn more about their experiences and successes.

> One of my goals with students is to increase their ability to orally share with their classmates information about literature characters and to inspire empathy about fictional characters' fatal flaws. So I allowed students to select books that interested them (we formed groups based on book selection), and I prompted them to carefully consider each character in the text. Students made meaning of the text by creating a Glogster poster that gave the most important stats and facts as well as having extended discussions within their groups about recurring themes. From there, each group held a counseling session in an attempt to remedy the character's fatal flaws. The audience (the rest of the class) had to listen to the session and use all the evidence available to determine if the diagnosis/recommendations were realistic. It was a great way for students to really consider their characters as complex people and express those ideas in an academic discussion.
>
> —Mary, High School English Teacher

> I was tired of my students' reading from PowerPoints every time I assigned them a presentation. So I used this instructional framework to help my students increase their ability to share a compelling message during a presentation. To begin, I modeled my expectations by sharing seven-minute mini-lessons on different topics in the curriculum. I tried to use stories and visuals to engage them. As I talked, I had students list the things I did that were effective and ineffective. From there, students selected their own seven-minute topics and created Prezis to supplement their talks. The Prezis could not include any words. Students provided feedback to one another using the rubric criteria from the framework. Many students commented that it was the first time they had actually had instruction on how to present better. Next time, I want to give the students authentic roles and problems for their presentations.
>
> —Jim, Ninth-Grade Teacher

Look Back and Step Forward

Delivering a compelling message to a specific audience is a skill that all students will need in their adult lives. The more opportunities teachers can give students to practice this competency thoughtfully and with specific feedback, the more refined their presentations will become!

A Question to Consider as You Reflect

How do we encourage students to truly be storytellers?

Going Viral

Common Core Standard Speaking and Listening Anchor Standard 5:
Make strategic use of digital media and visual displays of data to
express information and enhance understanding of presentations.

This Framework at a Glance

Framework Goals	• Create audio, images, or videos that share data effectively • Use digital media strategically when presenting information with regard to topic and audience
Tech Tools, Instructional Strategies, and Learning Activities	• Podbean (tech tool) www.podbean.com/. • Easel.ly (tech tool) www.easel.ly/. • Beginning, Middle, End Photos (instructional strategy) • Build a Graph (instructional strategy)
Final Assessment Options	• Infographic Mania • Podcast Digest • Share My Story
Criteria for Success on Final Assessment Options	• Overall Visual or Auditory Appeal • Relevance to Presentation Goals • Clarity of Message

How Can This Standard Build Student Competency in Content Areas?

As I shared in the last chapter, "Death by PowerPoint" just isn't cutting it anymore. Comedian Don McMillan pokes fun at the notion of ineffective media during presentations, seeking to remind us that even most people operating in the business world need to better communicate ideas visually. In his act, he cites moving text, too many bullets, and endless graphs as ways to simply annoy and confuse your audience.

Interestingly, Grant Wiggins compiled survey results from students across the United States relative to their likes and dislikes about school. One of the most hated activities, regardless of subject area or grade level, was "taking notes from a PowerPoint." When teachers simply deliver facts in a rote manner, it's not engaging (Wiggins, 2011).

So how can educators help students use images, sound, and videos to make impact as they deliver their arguments or stories? It begins with models. In Chapter 6, "Do-It-Yourself TED Talks," the framework exposes students to highly effective speakers and storytellers. As students begin to analyze and identify the strategies and techniques effective speakers use, they become more able to consider using these strategies themselves.

Students interact with media much more regularly than adults do. It is not uncommon for students to be listening to music, looking at pictures, and feebly attempting homework at the same time. Though scientific research has shown that such multitasking actually limits productivity and accuracy, students are very comfortable navigating the sea of media that exists in society today. Teachers can draw on these strengths to support the goals relative to the CCSS.

Given the viral nature of media today, it is critical for students to consider the types of images, sounds, and videos that will help them clarify and articulate their arguments while they present both formally and informally.

The ability to supplement ideas with compelling media is a skill that is absolutely essential for both college and career readiness. Therefore, this standard easily supports education's ultimate goal: graduating competent adults.

How Does This Standard Develop Across the K–12 Continuum?

The core component of this standard is the type of media that should be generated by the student and the purpose for which it should be used during a presentation. Students at the early elementary levels should use simple drawings or audio to support their ideas, while students at the high school level should strategically generate and employ all different types of media during presentations. Personally, I believe students should have opportunities to generate digital media, regardless of their grade level. Consider that when making decisions about the instructional implementation of this framework. Consider Figure 8.1 (page 116).

This standard demands that students both understand a topic and express it carefully using different forms of media. Students begin this process naturally, using drawings to amplify and clarify stories about their lives. From there, students begin to craft compelling presentations complete with a variety of media formats that will engage the audience at hand. In short, the areas of spiraling complexity within the standard are these:

♦ The types of media created and used (from drawings to interactive elements)
♦ The purpose for media use (from adding detail to enhancing understanding)

About the Instructional Design Framework

This instructional design framework is titled "Going Viral." In today's culture, many different kinds of media go "viral." This means they are repeated, reshared, and remixed through a variety of different media. It also means people are talking about them, formally and informally. This framework will help students create images, audio, and videos that support the main points within presentations or stories. Depending on your subject area and the age of your students, you may introduce your students to infographics, podcasts, or graphs using the activities shared in

Figure 8.1 What Media Students Should Effectively Use When Presenting

When presenting formally or informally, students should effectively use . . .		
Grade	**Media Type**	**Purpose for Use**
K	Drawings	To provide additional detail
1	Drawings	To clarify ideas, thoughts, or feelings
2	Drawings or audio recordings	To clarify ideas, thoughts, or feelings
3	Audio recordings or visual displays	To emphasize or enhance certain details
4	Audio recordings or visual displays	To enhance the development of main ideas or themes
5	Multimedia components (graphics, sound) or visual displays	To enhance the development of main ideas or themes
6	Multimedia components (graphics, images, music, sound) or visual displays	To clarify information
7	Multimedia components (graphics, images, music, sound) or visual displays	To clarify claims and findings and emphasize salient points
8	Multimedia components (graphics, images, music, sound) or visual displays	To clarify information, strengthen claims, and add interest
9–10	Digital media (textual, graphical, audio, visual, and interactive elements)	To enhance understanding of findings and add interest
11–12	Digital media (textual, graphical, audio, visual, and interactive elements)	To enhance understanding of findings and add interest

this framework. As students create media throughout the framework, they should always be clear about the purpose for using the media as well as the impact the media will make on the audience.

Logic and accuracy are also important. Students should use data to help them communicate a story, main message, or argument.

This framework will provide students with opportunities to "play" with different media formats to help them emphasize and clarify important messages. Encourage students to test their designs on peers and friends. Students need real-time feedback on the strategies and formats that most effectively draw a response from the audience. (In truth, this is a challenging task as a practiced adult!)

Any content area can find connections to this instructional design framework because multimedia relates to any field or topic. Just make sure the topics you select are engaging for students.

Framework Goals
◆   Create audio, images, or videos that share data effectively
◆   Use digital media strategically when presenting information with regard to topic and audience

Tech Tools, Instructional Strategies, and Learning Activities

This standard requires students to generate pieces of multimedia that support their speeches and presentations. When experimenting with different types of media, students should be encouraged to embrace an atmosphere of play. The best way for students to become comfortable using media flexibly is to have them experiment and create in a positive, free atmosphere. To encourage this type of creation, two tech tools and two instructional strategies are shared relative to Standard 5.

Podbean (tech tool)
Podbean is a place where you can create and share podcasts for free. Given the emphasis on audio recordings in grades 2 through 4, this tool is a great fit for students at those levels. With Podbean, students can create podcasts peers or parents can subscribe to. Having a podcast channel for your classroom is a great way to provide regular opportunities for students to produce meaningful work that is shared with a large audience. One thing

to note is that young students may require supervision or direct links when using the Podbean site. There are lots of different podcasts available, and all topics may not be suitable for young children. To get started with Podbean, follow these four easy steps:

1. Go to www.podbean.com.
2. Register and get an account.
3. Upload your recordings to your new channel.
4. Share!

Podbean has a large collection of educational podcasts and classroom podcasts. (See the directory for educational podcasts here: www.podbean .com/podcasts?s=hit&c=education&t=month&p=1.) This tool can be used with any content area at any level. Here are a few I noted:

♦ "Little Reviews" is a podcast created to help young students learn about new books. You can visit it here: www.podbean.com/podcast-detail?pid=5562.

♦ The Seattle Public Library produces a "Podcast for Teens" to help teens learn about cutting-edge books and programs. You can listen to it here: www.podbean.com/podcast-detail?pid=151419.

♦ Cinco Ranch High School shares weekly school updates with the public on its podcast site here: www.podbean.com/podcast-detail ?pid=42040.

♦ The Aurora School Board publishes the audio of all board meetings on its podcast site: auroraschoolboard.podbean.com/.

♦ A first-grade teacher has students practice their fluency by recording their "best reading presentations" to a podcast site. Students are very excited to have friends and family hear their smooth reading!

♦ A middle school teacher charges several of her students with the weekly announcements for their class. Students have to summarize the most important learning from the week and share it in a funny, engaging way. This is the most sought-after extra assignment in the school!

♦ A high school guidance counselor has students create three-minute podcasts about their "first days in high school." The podcast channel is shared with incoming freshman on the first day of school, aiding their transition to a large, bustling building of learning.

Easel.ly (tech tool)

Easel.ly is an infographic generator that is completely web based. (That means you don't have to download anything to use it.) This program already has lots of templates and clip art available, so it helps students to get to work quickly. An extensive gallery of completed infographics can help students identify techniques that work well and techniques that fall flat. Easel.ly also has many different options for sharing finished work, ranging from simple pdf downloads to many different social media sites, such as Twitter. See the example in Figure 8.2 from a recent professional development project I completed. To get started with Easel.ly, follow these five easy steps:

1. Go to www.easel.ly/.
2. Click the "register" button, and create an account.
3. Click on the template that works for you.
4. Rearrange the text and images as you see fit.
5. Share your work!

Figure 8.2 Example of Easel.ly

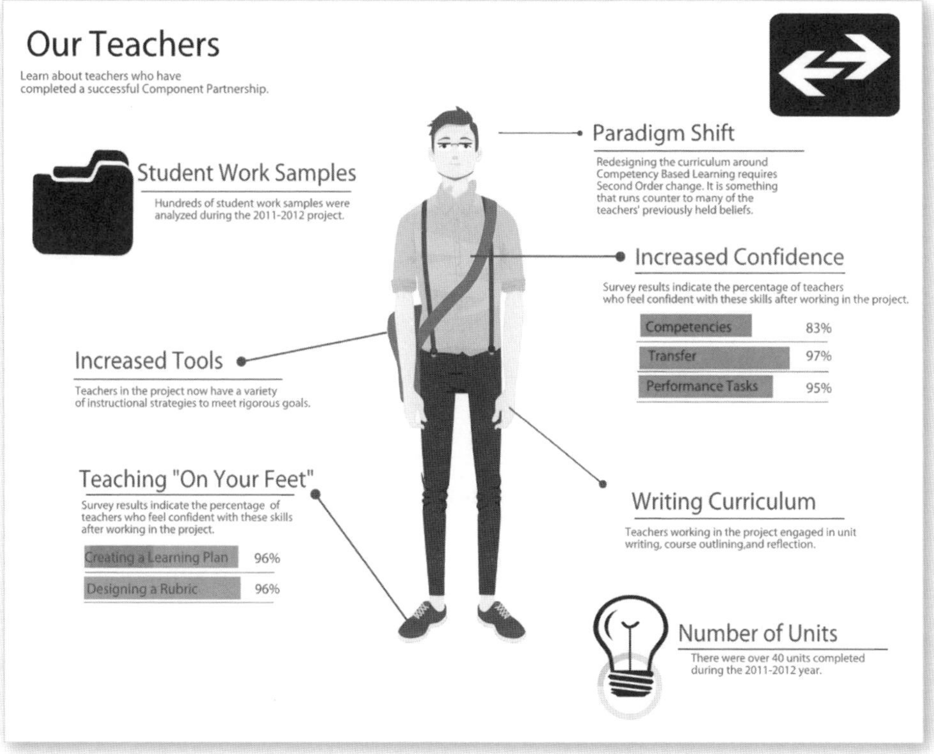

Easel.ly works well with any subject area or grade level. Students can create lots of different visuals that express meaning through size, text, art, and arrangement.

◆   An elementary teacher works with her class to create an infographic about the number of birthdays that occur each month. Students use different-sized cakes to represent the number of birthdays. Students have to think carefully to arrange the cakes in a clear, visually appealing manner. Students present and explain the infographic to the school nurse so she can better anticipate which months will be busy for annual vision checkups.

◆   A middle school teacher has students create yes-no flowcharts using questions reflective of different characters in *The Hunger Games*. Students design the infographics so participants will answer questions that tell if they are more inclined to befriend Katniss, Peeta, or Gale. Students present their infographics to the class and elicit feedback from their peers.

◆   A high school chemistry teacher has his students create different infographics about regions of the periodic table. Students have to think about the important properties within a region and express the information in a striking way. Students then use the infographics during informal jigsaw presentations to the entire class.

Beginning, Middle, and End Photos (instructional strategy)

Using media to tell a story can come naturally to students if the media can be connected to their personal experiences. This instructional strategy helps students use media strategically during presentations about things they experienced. It is most closely aligned with Standard 5 in grades 1 through 4. It requires students to craft their presentations as "stories," complete with a beginning, a middle, and an end. Most early elementary classrooms use this structure during the writing process. Integrating this language into the presentation process strengthens students' understanding of an organized, logical presentation with a strategic deployment of images.

Try these four steps to use this strategy in your classroom:

1.   Begin by modeling the process for students. Depending on the students who are experiencing the lesson, you may wish to use images from a recent story or classroom experience. Tell a story

with a distinct beginning, middle, and end. Show them three images. The first image should show the beginning of the story. The second image should show the middle of the story. The third and final image should show the end of a story. Reference each photo at the appropriate time.

2. Next, students create their own stories. They can choose to take photographs, bring photographs from home, or draw pictures of the beginning, middle, and end of their stories, which are actually their presentations.

3. Glue the photographs onto large paper, and label each photograph as beginning, middle, or end.

4. Have students share their stories (or presentations) with the class, and have their peers ask clarifying questions as needed.

This strategy is commonly used with elementary students, and the images serve as both prompts and strategic clarifiers. When used in the older grades, this strategy requires that students have confidence and mastery of their topics, as "reading from the slides" is impossible when using this strategy.

♦ A first-grade teacher has students draw the beginning, middle, and end of their favorite Eric Carle stories. Students have to retell the stories for their peers using their images.

♦ A fifth-grade teacher has students take photographs while on a class field trip to a stream. Students arrange the photographs in clusters of beginning, middle, and end. Then students recount the experience to the fourth-grade students, who will attend the trip the following year.

♦ A high school social studies teacher wants to eradicate presentations in which students simply read bullet points from a Power-Point presentation. To amend this, he tells students they have to find three historical photographs about a particular topic in history. (Photographs could be political cartoons, actual still shots, or drawings.) Students have to share their information while referencing the three images. This helps students stay focused while remaining cognizant of the "story" aspect within historical events.

Build a Graph (instructional strategy)

Graphs are one of the most commonly used media forms shared in formal presentations. However, they are often confusing, difficult to read,

Figure 8.3 Fat Consumed

or misleading. This strategy helps students consider the message their graphs should impart. Once students determine the idea a graph should communicate, they actually build (out of physical objects) a graph. Students display their graphs in the classroom during their presentations as impactful reminders of the logical data that supports their arguments or presentations. For example, a third-grade class uses deflated playground balls to show how many balls were kicked over the train tracks each month. After the formal presentation to the principal, the graph is displayed in the hallway of the school to remind students to kick *more gently*. Figure 8.3 shows a graph built by Jamie Oliver to show students how much fat they eat. (He actually brought a truckload of animal fat to the school. What a graph to show size and magnitude!)

Try these six steps to use this strategy in your classroom:

1. Have students create purpose statements for their graphs. You can use the following sentence starter: *The point of my graph is to . . .*
2. Students should share the purpose statements with at least three peers to ensure that they are compelling.
3. Next, students should collect the information they need to make their graphs.
4. Students should sketch the graphs on paper. This should simply be a way to record the data for future reference.
5. Students should select engaging materials from which to build their graphs. Graphs can be large or small, depending on the audience and presentation setting.

6. Students should build their graphs and use them during their presentations.

This strategy is a great way of integrating the emotional impact of art with speaking and listening. By starting with a purpose statement, students ensure that the role of the graphs in their presentations is clear and concise. Impact is heightened by the selection and use of interesting materials. This strategy can be used at any level with any subject. Again, viewing this task as an integration of cold hard data and emotional art is an excellent way to help students see the connections among many different disciplines.

- A second-grade teacher has students use broken pencil points to represent the number of times a student has to sharpen his or her pencil during a single week. Once the students create the graph, they present different ways to reduce the number of broken pencil points. During each presentation, students reference the graph.
- Students from a high school current events class collect battered sneakers to represent the number of high school students living at shelters in various communities throughout their school district. Students referenced their large graph while presenting to the school board about the need to eliminate a pay-to-play program.
- Students in a middle school social studies class are exploring the quality and value of Wikipedia as a research source. To help explain some of their points, they stack erasers to show how many changes are made to several popular Wikipedia pages on an average day. After presenting their findings to the school librarian, students display the graph in the library to pique the curiosity of all middle school students.

Formative Assessment and Student Progress Tracking

Creating images, sound, and videos that emphasize and support the main points of a presentation is a vital skill for students who plan to enter today's knowledge-based economy. As students experiment with different forms of media, they need feedback to help them determine which forms work most effectively with various audiences.

In many cases, instant feedback occurs when enacting many things contained within the speaking and listening standards. For example, if you tell a humorous personal story and people laugh, you have feedback that your story was, in fact, funny. If you present a business pitch to potential investors and they opt to invest, you have feedback that your presentation was successful.

However, when different forms of media are used during a presentation, the feedback can be a bit veiled. It may be hard for the presenter to gauge an audience's reaction to a carefully crafted chart or image. Teacher and directed peer guidance can be very helpful in this area. Students need others to view their media and ask questions about it. Often these questions will help them identify ways to improve their work. What's confusing? What does this image make you think? Those questions can help students move their work forward.

As always, remember to be transparent about the learning stage required for each task (i.e., acquisition, meaning making, and transfer). The more students can recognize the cognitive demand and independence required, the more likely they will be successful!

Consider Figure 8.4 from a fifth-grade science teacher. She wants her students to present their findings from a self-designed science experiment using at least three photos, graphs, or images from their work. ELA and science standards are integrated to ensure a seamless feedback mechanism for students in all areas of the task.

Instructional Framework Final Assessment: Evidence of Goal Achievement

The final assessment selections for this instructional framework require students to remix media in ways that support main ideas contained within their presentations. Students should be able to analyze their messages and create interesting media they can reference during their presentations. Students must rise above the endless PowerPoint bullets seen in many dry presentations.

Each final assessment option focuses on a different type of media: images, audio, and videos. If desired, you may choose to integrate these different options to encourage students to synthesize different types of media. (Such remixing is becoming increasingly popular.)

As always, feel free to make adjustments to these assessment options to meet the needs of your students. As long as the rigor of the task is not sacrificed, you can adjust these tasks in many different ways!

Figure 8.4 Student Progress Tracking

Standard	Behavior(s)	Learning Stage	Evidence/Attempts Toward Mastery			Notes/Feedback
Common Core Standard Speaking and Listening Anchor Standard 5: Make strategic use of digital media and visual displays of data to express information and enhance understanding of presentations.	Use two photos and one graph during a presentation about a science experiment.	Transfer				
	Use photos and graphs to clarify and augment the main conclusion of the report.	Transfer				

Figure 8.4 Student Progress Tracking (continued)

Standard	Behavior(s)	Learning Stage	Evidence/Attempts Toward Mastery				Notes/Feedback
NJ Science Standard 5.1.8.B.2 Gather, evaluate, and represent evidence using scientific tools, technologies, and computational strategies.	Take photos of the experiment design that illuminate key steps.	Meaning making or inferencing					
	Know the names of different scientific tools and technologies in order to appropriately label photographs.	Acquisition					
	Create graphs from data sets.	Meaning making or inferencing					

Final Assessment Option 1: Infographic Mania

You are a graphic designer for a web-based start-up company on the West Coast. One of your most fickle clients has requested an infographic to show the growth of its company. (You can tailor the nature of the client to the specific subject area you teach. For example, a social studies teacher may select the Pony Express.) As the graphic designer, you need to research the growth of the company and use an infographic to explain this information to both the client and consumers. This infographic will be used in the client's first-quarter statements to all the employees in the company. Be prepared to present your infographic to the client and explain how it carefully and clearly shares an important message. Also be prepared to answer any questions that may arise.

Connections
Anchor Standards for Speaking and Listening: 1, 6
Anchor Standard for Reading: 1
Anchor Standards for Writing: 6, 7

Final Assessment Option 2: Podcast Digest

You are a news reporter who is responsible for informing the general community about the happenings at your school or classroom. You must create a two-minute podcast updating the general community about everything that has happened in your school/classroom. Your delivery will be very important if you want to hold the listeners' interest. Consider using sound effects or jingles to catch the attention of your listeners as well. Your podcast will be posted to the podcast channel that houses local news.

Connections
Anchor Standard for Speaking and Listening: 6
Anchor Standard for Writing: 6

Final Assessment Option 3: Share My Story

You work for a documentary director. He has demanded a three-minute clip of a person (or student) telling a favorite personal story. (You can change the nature of the story to better suit your content area. For example, in science you may ask students to share their personal experiences with gravity.) You must collect the footage for the clip and share it with your director. Unfortunately, you waited until the last minute to complete this assignment. Now you must feature *yourself* in the video. Figure out your compelling story, record it, and share it. Be prepared to explain why your video meets the demands of the director.

Connections
Anchor Standards for Speaking and Listening: 1, 6
Anchor Standard for Writing: 6

Final Assessment Rubric Guidance

You may wish to adapt the rubric criteria in Figure 8.5 to fit the needs of your students and your situation. Only the highest level is provided in an effort to help you focus on the end goal as described by the standard.

Suggestions for Differentiation

The general diversity of media allows for a significant amount of differentiation within this framework. In the real world, all formal and informal presenters use many different types of media. Often, a presenter's choice of media is related to personal preferences and experiences. To this end, teachers can provide students with lots of different options!

1. Allow students to choose what type of media they use in their presentations. You may also want to provide students with a menu of tech tools they can use to generate media. The greater the level of student choice, the more likely teachers are to reach students at their level of readiness.
2. Require different numbers of media artifacts in a given presentation. For example, some students may need to include an infographic and a thirty-second film, while others may need to include only a graph. Especially because some forms of media take a significant amount of time to generate, this differentiation can help alleviate the burden on students who tend to work slowly.
3. Provide students with scaffolds. For example, you can provide students with a template for a graph that they complete. Or, you can provide students with a template for an infographic that they complete. However, if you opt for this strategy, you must ensure that students have a clear understanding of the purpose and

Figure 8.5 Rubric Criteria

Rubric Indicator	A Description of Capstone Performance
Overall Visual or Auditory Appeal	• If the artifact is an image, it is visually appealing to the audience. • If the artifact is an image, it can be read clearly by the audience. • If the artifact is auditory, it is clearly understood with effective pacing and inflection.
Relevance to the Presentation Goals	• The media selected or created is directly aligned to presentation goals. • The media selected or created uses words, sounds, or information that is aligned with the needs of the audience. • The media is used at an appropriate time during the presentation, and its inclusion does not seem choppy.
Clarity of Message	• The intended message of the media is clearly received by the audience during the presentation.

message of their media. If not, you have reduced the level of rigor, and students will not meet the demands of Standard 5.

4. Ask students to design their own differentiation. Hold them to a high standard of rigor.

Window Into the Classroom

Jane, a fifth-grade teacher, had students design their own science experiments every year. Traditionally, students loved the assignment, and they shared their results during a class celebration that parents and peers attended. However, Jane wanted to revise the presentation component of the project to include some different media sources. So Jane required students to create three different types of media to share during the class celebration. To ensure that students were successful in this endeavor, she added a series of learning activities to the end of her unit to ensure that students had a series of tools at their disposal. Consider the following sequence:

◆ **Learning Activity:** After students completed their self-designed experiments, Jane introduced the class to Easel.ly. At first, students learned to use the tool. Then students created infographics that summed up the most important results from their experiments. Essentially, students needed to make graphical images of what they discovered through their experiments.

◆ **Learning Activity:** Next, Jane had students record thirty-second audio clips detailing the procedure used in their experiments. She encouraged students to rerecord their audio clips until they were satisfied with their cadence and clarity. These clips will be used during the final assessment.

◆ **Learning Activity:** Students took photographs of different elements of their scientific experiments. These photographs included steps in the procedures that were very critical, elements of the results, or scientific tools that were needed for the experiments. Students needed to ensure that the photographs they took were closely related to the main ideas they wanted to share in their upcoming science celebration.

◆ **Final Assessment:** Jane decided to combine several of the different options outlined in the instructional framework for her final assessment. She wanted students to use the infographic, audio, and photographs they had created or taken during her instructional sequence. Students had to put these artifacts into coherent order and reference them strategically during their presentations in the upcoming science celebration. Everyone at the celebration completed a slip that said, "The most important thing I learned from this presentation was . . ." This helped students collect feedback about the alignment between their presentations and their results.

At the end of the learning experience, Jane felt very proud of the student presentations at the science celebration. The students were able to use a variety of media sources to make their brief presentations informative, entertaining, and on topic.

However, Jane saw weaknesses in the infographics that students created. Many were too flashy to clearly communicate a single message. She planned to revisit this task with a later unit on microorganisms in an effort to provide students with additional opportunities to refine their skills in this area.

Teacher Perspectives

For this instructional framework, two teachers across the United States adapted these ideas to their specific needs and situations. Read on to learn more about their experiences and successes.

I noticed that many of my students were not using visuals effectively during their presentations in school. In fact, many of them were quickly skipping past images and maps and spending more time on slides crowded with bulleted text. I took a few pieces of this framework to help students consider what engaging visuals could look like during a presentation. First, I showed them different infographics from both the Easel.ly site and CNN. Then I asked them to consider how these images told a story and shared a point. To make meaning of what I shared, students were told to bring in powerful images they found in their travels over a weekend. (Students' brought in a variety of different things, including toy circulars and company budget reports.) Finally, I told students to use their learning and the evaluative criteria shared in this framework to evaluate different speakers during our field trip to the Robotics Fair. This resulted in some great takeaways for students. Over the next few months, I want to integrate this learning into their capstone presentation project at our school.

—Jill, Middle School Teacher

I tried this entire framework with Final Assessment Option 1: Infographic Mania. We used our unit on ancient Egypt for the content. My students really wanted to make their own infographics, and engagement was high. I videotaped their final presentations/pitches and shared them with other teachers. It was a great success!

—Todd, Fourth-Grade Teacher

Look Back and Step Forward

A strategic use of media is challenging. Allowing students to experiment with both the creation and deployment of different types of media is very important. This instructional framework provides you with lots of ideas for cultivating this important competency.

A Question to Consider as You Reflect

How can students create media that supports their points and makes their message sticky?

Language as Currency ⑨

Common Core Standard Speaking and Listening Anchor Standard 6:
Adapt speech to a variety of contexts and communicative
tasks, demonstrating command of formal English
when indicated or appropriate.

This Framework at a Glance

Framework Goals	• Select words and sentences that meet the needs of the audience when speaking • Self-monitor personal speech in formal and informal situations
Tech Tools, Instructional Strategies, and Learning Activities	• instaGrok (tech tool) www.instagrok.com/ • Gotbrainy (tech tool) www.gotbrainy.com • Tier Word Selection Framework (instructional strategy)
Final Assessment Options	• Pinwheel Discussions • Vocabulary Cartoon • Specifying Student Roles During Discussion
Criteria for Success on Final Assessment Options	• Word Choice • Pacing and Flow • Grammar

How Can This Standard Build Student Competency in Content Areas?

If you've ever had the chance to listen to teens or preteens in a mall or movie theater, it's quite possible that the conversation went something like this (this excerpt was actually overheard in a suburban mall near a McDonald's):

> "No, like, it was totally cool."
> "Did she, like, uh, like it?"
> "Yeah, it was, like, def."
> "Yeah. Uh. Cool."
> "Cool."

Though students may be incredibly intelligent and thoughtful, many of their informal conversations employ endless "likes," "ums," and "yeahs." Given this, educators must explicitly teach students how to speak in both formal and informal settings. Students must be able to use language that is accepted by the audience. Otherwise, their message may be compromised by the words they use. This can be challenging, especially in on-demand situations such as presentations, panels, or job interviews. Considerable practice is likely required.

Notably, there is a sizable difference between speaking to share learning and speaking to process new content. Teachers must honor students' speech in all forms when they are using language to generate understanding of a new topic. However, once they have mastered an idea, they must be able to self-monitor their language as they share it with a wide variety of audiences.

Further, Standard 6 permeates all the other standards in the Common Core Speaking and Listening Standards domain. Students have to self-monitor their language, and they have to be very self-aware to use words that will meet the needs of their audience. It is a competency that develops over time in response to increased speaking experience. Therefore, the nature of this standard demands that teachers provide students with many opportunities to speak in both formal and informal settings.

Meeting this standard in all academic disciplines requires students to be aware of the language nuances that exist. For example, teachers share a unique vocabulary that includes "differentiated instruction," "achievement," and "individualized education plans." Those who want to communicate with us professionally in formal settings must be aware of those vocabulary words and be able to respond to them thoughtfully. It follows, therefore, that teachers need to help students uncover the words and phrases that professionals use in different academic disciplines. Many researchers and educators have referred to these words as academic vocabulary.

Allowing students to become poised when using language is a competency that will serve them throughout college and life. Therefore, this standard easily supports education's ultimate goal: graduating competent adults.

How Does This Standard Develop Across the K–12 Continuum?

The focal point of this standard is actually embedded in the Common Core Standards for ELA. Standard 6 demands that as students mature, they use vocabulary and grammatical structures appropriate to their grade level—for example, moving from simple sentences to more complex structures. Additionally, students must select words that accurately describe their ideas for the intended audience. Due to this, the standard remains the same throughout most of the K–12 continuum. Consider the redundancy in Figure 9.1 (page 136).

This standard demands that students speak with the poise and tenor required for formal situations. The rigor of this standard increases as the language and grammar required at a particular grade level or grade band increase. In short, the areas of spiraling complexity within the standard are these:

- ♦ The shift from simply stating full sentences to using adaptive speech in the later grades
- ♦ The sophistication of language, word choice, and grammar demanded in speech

About the Instructional Design Framework

This instructional framework is titled "Language as Currency." The word *currency* is used to indicate that language is something you use to buy credibility when interacting in formal situations. Given this, the framework

Figure 9.1 Actions Students Should Take When Presenting

When presenting formally or informally, students should . . .		
Grade	Action	Qualifier
K	Speak audibly and express thoughts	With clarity
1	Produce full sentences	When appropriate to task and situation
2	Produce full sentences	When appropriate to task and situation and to provide requested detail or clarification
3	Produce full sentences	When appropriate to task and situation and to provide requested detail or clarification
4	Differentiate between contexts that call for formal English and situations where informal discourse is appropriate	When appropriate to task and situation and to provide requested detail or clarification

encourages students to collect words, phrases, and demeanors that translate into formal settings.

In many ways, this chapter is more of an instructional supplement than a complete framework. Students should be able to differentiate between formal and informal contexts, but this cannot be done in isolation. Further, the content area will dictate which academic vocabulary is required to reach the audience. Therefore, this framework is best used as a way of enriching and refining your current practices. In short, use the framework in conjunction with other frameworks or units you already teach.

The goals allow students to explore language relative to an academic discipline to determine the phrases that will be required in a formal presentation given the audience's level of expertise. Encourage students to explore the ways a particular discipline or group of people use language to make specific connections to practices, ideas, or theories. These skills will certainly go a long way for students throughout their lives!

Figure 9.1 Actions Students Should Take When Presenting (continued)

Grade	Action	Qualifier
5	Adapt speech to a variety of contexts and tasks	When appropriate to task and situation
6	Adapt speech to a variety of contexts and tasks	Demonstrating a command of formal English when appropriate
7	Adapt speech to a variety of contexts and tasks	Demonstrating a command of formal English when appropriate
8	Adapt speech to a variety of contexts and tasks	Demonstrating a command of formal English when appropriate
9–10	Adapt speech to a variety of contexts and tasks	Demonstrating a command of formal English when appropriate
11–12	Adapt speech to a variety of contexts and tasks	Demonstrating a command of formal English when appropriate

Framework Goals

- Select words and sentences that meet the needs of the audience when speaking
- Self-monitor personal speech in formal and informal situations

Tech Tools, Instructional Strategies, and Learning Activities

This standard requires students to explore the connections that exist within the academic vocabulary used by a particular academic discipline. When helping students uncover these words and ideas, you must aid students in connecting this learning to what they already know. Whether they create visuals, practice with a peer, or draft graphic organizers, students must make the language their own. To encourage this type of ownership, two tech tools and one instructional strategy are shared relative to Standard 6.

instaGrok (tech tool)

The search engine instaGrok displays results using a series of webbed bubbles. Related topics and connections are made very explicit when using this tool. Sites such as instaGrok that provide this service are sometimes called visual search engines. This tool is linked to Standard 6 because it can help students build academic vocabulary regarding particular topics or ideas. Students should search words related to their topics to generate related lists of academic vocabulary. This site is a great context-building tool for students. To get started with instaGrok, follow these four easy steps:

1. Go to www.instagrok.com.
2. Input your search term on the home page.
3. Review the results in "graph mode."
4. Create a list of academic vocabulary related to your topic.

This tool is suitable for many different types of students. Consider the examples below:

♦ A second-grade teacher uses the tool to search the "word of the day" each day. After viewing the word and words related to it, students create a quick sketch of all the items or ideas related to the word. Students share their sketches with a partner using full sentences. It takes only a few minutes, and it helps them refine both their cognitive schema and their academic vocabulary relative to a topic.

♦ A fifth-grade teacher has students create their own vocabulary lists by skimming three science trade books on biomes. Once students have identified the words, they put each word into insta-Grok. Students have to create a web to show how the selected words are related (if they are related). This helps students identify and understand the vocabulary required for formal discourse on the topic of biomes.

♦ A seventh-grade teacher uses instaGrok as a way to check for understanding regarding students' grasp of academic vocabulary related to an introductory unit on economics. She shows students the web without revealing the word she searched. By viewing the graphic organizer, students have to determine a word that fits and defend their assertions. This leads to an interesting discussion about the types of language used in the discipline.

♦ A ninth-grade librarian helps her students identify academic search terms about a topic. After selecting their topics, students input the terms into instaGrok. Students use the webbed suggestions to create at least fifteen search terms they can use in academic databases. This helps them build a formal language to use when learning about and discussing their research topics formally and informally.

Gotbrainy (tech tool)

Gotbrainy is a social community for students who are learning and processing new vocabulary. The site focuses specifically on vocabulary words that transcend academic disciplines and make up substantial portions of academic texts. (Think of words such as *ubiquitous*, *divisive*, and *plethora*.) Students can gain facility with these words by reviewing the visual cartoons (usually a combination of stunning photos and witty captions) or creating their own. I've used this site with high school sophomores to help them understand their science textbooks. The students enjoyed the site so much, they started submitting photos for fun! To get started with Gotbrainy, follow these three easy steps:

1. Go to www.gotbrainy.com/.
2. Surf or search the words on the site.
3. Register and create an account if you'd like to submit your own captioned images to the site!

Gotbrainy is a community best suited for middle school and high school students due to the dictionary of words on the site, but the concept can be used with any level. Students of any age can snap a photo and put a caption to it!

♦ A middle school ELA teacher has students submit two vocabulary words to the site each month. The words are generated by the students, not a text or compendium. Because of this routine, students begin thinking about the words differently and incorporating new words more authentically into their speech, both formally and informally.

♦ A high school science teacher has students take pictures of a lab experiment that uses Bunsen burners. Students select academic vocabulary words, write witty captions, and submit them to the site. The students enjoy this practice so much, they request using it more often. Students really enjoy seeing their work displayed within the community and search out new words to exemplify their intense laboratory pictures. (Just imagine the fun they have with the pig dissection lab!)

♦ A middle school physical education teacher has students photograph different sports throughout the year. Then students use academic vocabulary words from their English literature class to caption the images and submit them to the community. It is an excellent interdisciplinary, problem-solving experience. Students use formal language to present their work.

Tier Word Selection Framework (instructional strategy)

The Tier Word Selection Framework comes from research by Beck, McKeown, and Kucan in 2002. Essentially, the strategy lays out three different types of vocabulary words students can encounter during instruction.

Tier 1 words are words that can be easily conceptualized. You can show students a picture of the word, or the word is used in common conversations. Consider words such as *red*, *brick*, etc.

Tier 2 words are words that serve as the "mortar" of academic discussion and the formal English language. These words tend to glue together formal conversation, and they are often used in a variety of disciplines or subject areas. Think of such words as *fortunate*, *sizable*, and *era*.

Tier 3 words tend to be the words on the traditional vocabulary lists in different subjects. These words may be helpful when understanding a specific topic, but these words don't tend to be used outside the subject at hand. Consider words such as *biome*, *macroeconomics*, and *capitalization*.

This strategy requires you to consider the three tiers of words when identifying the language that is important for students to acquire. When helping students develop the language that will serve as currency in formal presentation settings, tier 2 words tend to provide the largest impact.

You can share these tiers with students and even have students categorize different words using the framework. Try these three steps to use this strategy in your classroom:

1. Begin by modeling the process for students. Show students a list of words, and demonstrate which words go into each tier. For younger students, you may want to rename the categories with words that are more familiar (for example, "easy things," "sticky glue words," and "expensive words").

2. Next have students generate words from a text, topic, or body of study you are doing. This can happen over a period of days or weeks. It should be a natural process.

3. Finally, have students categorize the words they are using into different tiers. Students should focus on incorporating tier 2 words into their formal language. These words can be posted throughout the year and referenced when students give formal presentations.

This strategy can be used in any subject area or grade level. Here are some ways teachers use this strategy to help students develop a heightened awareness of the ways that vocabulary impacts their spoken language and writing:

♦ A kindergarten teacher collects and celebrates "fancy" (tier 2) words and puts them on a large pearl necklace display in the classroom. Students try to use these words in their spoken language and writing.

♦ A seventh-grade teacher has students generate a list of "interesting" words using primary source documents about a historical topic. Then students sort the words into tier 1, tier 2, and tier 3. When students give their presentations at the end of the unit, they try to incorporate as many tier 2 words as they can.

♦ A high school science teacher provides students with tiered vocabulary lists. Students are not required to memorize any tier 1 or tier 3 words. Instead, the teacher provides these on index cards for reference. Alternatively, tier 2 words are actively practiced, prioritized, and assessed.

Formative Assessment and Student Progress Tracking

Monitoring one's speech to ensure it is appropriate in formal settings can be extremely difficult. Especially in the beginning, substantial teacher feedback is required. I once watched a middle school teacher work with students in a small group to eradicate "ums" and "yeahs." Arriving at smooth, uninterrupted speech took between ten and fifteen tries. Although the activity was fun and the students were laughing like crazy, the feedback was necessary.

When trying to utilize formal English, instant feedback is really important. Practicing with a critical peer can also assist the process. When helping students meet goals within Standard 6, provide them with clear models and rubrics to assess their work. Be sure students are aware of the learning stage as well. If students know they are in acquisition, meaning-making, or transfer modes, then they can employ strategic actions to be successful. Students need explicit expectations, and they also need to monitor their progress along the way. Even the tiniest improvements should be celebrated!

Consider the example in Figure 9.2 from seventh-grade language arts and science teachers. The team wanted students to identify the vocabulary from the field of botany. The two teachers wanted to help students use formal English when sharing and learning about the topic.

Instructional Framework Final Assessment: Evidence of Goal Achievement

As I noted in the beginning of this chapter, Standard 6 is best achieved when taught in conjunction with a host of other standards from rigorous content areas such as social studies or science as well as other Common Core Standards for ELA. So, a final assessment of Standard 6 in isolation is not the best way to measure achievement of this standard for students. Therefore, I will share three action-packed tasks that may incorporate other standards for this framework. I will note those connections with each task.

As you review each task presented here, you may also want to consider adapting the task for regular classroom use. Instead of employing one option a single time, how could you create structures in your classroom that allow these options to be regular practices? This would certainly provide you with a more complete picture of student performance over time.

Be sure to consider the needs of your students as you review each option. You are the designer of the assessment experience for your students.

Final Assessment Option 1: Pinwheel Discussions

Pinwheel discussions allow students to participate in and listen to high-level discussions. First, students have to generate important discussion questions about the topic at hand. These questions should be complex, open-ended questions that do not have a single correct answer. (This makes a great homework assignment!) Then students set up their desks into a pinwheel formation. (Four desks face each other and a row of desks follows

Figure 9.2 Student Progress Tracking

Standard	Behavior(s)	Learning Stage	Evidence/Attempts Toward Mastery		Notes/Feedback
Common Core Standard Speaking and Listening Anchor Standard 6: Adapt speech to a variety of contexts and communicative tasks, demonstrating command of formal English when indicated or appropriate.	Identify formal language in the field of botany.	Acquisition			
	Use formal words and speech when sharing about the topic of botany during class discussions.	Meaning making or inferencing			

Figure 9.2 Student Progress Tracking (continued)

Standard	Behavior(s)	Learning Stage	Evidence/Attempts Toward Mastery	Notes/Feedback
PA Science Standard S7.B.1.1.2 Describe how specific structures in living things (from cell to organism) help them function effectively in specific ways (e.g., chlorophyll in plant cells—photosynthesis; root hairs—increased surface area; beak structures in birds—food gathering; cacti spines—protection from predators).	Identify the key parts of plants.	Acquisition		
	Explain the functions of the different parts of a plant.	Meaning making or inferencing		
	Evaluate the parts of the plant that enable it to survive in harsh conditions.	Transfer		

Figure 9.3 Pinwheel Formation of Desks

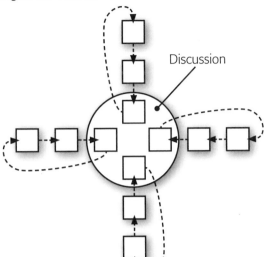

Discussion

behind. See Figure 9.3.) One group of students is designated as the moderators. These students ask questions and guide group discussion. Some modeling of this task may be required the first time you do this. Students at the center of the room (sitting at the four "head desks") begin the discussion. After a short time, a moderator tells the students who are having the discussion to pass. These students go to the end of their rows, and new students move up to the head desks. This allows students to participate in as well as hear discussion about complex topics. As students engage in the task, you should be taking notes about the discussion. Are students using formal English? Are they using the vocabulary expected in the discipline? This structure and assessment is completely student driven, works with lots of different subject areas, and is appropriate for almost every grade level. (In younger grade levels, the teacher may want to serve as the moderator at first.) It is an excellent structure to monitor the inclusion of formal English and rigorous vocabulary when students are expressing their ideas orally.

Note: If you want to make this task more authentic, assign roles to students. For example, if you are discussing a text from ELA, have each student take on the role of a character from the text.

Connections
Anchor Standards for Speaking and Listening: 1, 4
Anchor Standard for Reading: 1

Final Assessment Option 2: Vocabulary Cartoon

You are a cartoonist. It is your job to create an image that includes at least five different tier 2 vocabulary words that you, the cartoonist, have learned throughout your studies. (This should be related to a specific body of study or content unit in your classroom.) Once you have created the cartoon, you must present it to the newspaper editor for approval. You must explain the words you selected and how you depicted them. During your presentation, be sure to use language that is appropriate for your *very serious boss*. If your cartoon is approved, it will be printed in the newspaper and posted on Gotbrainy!

Connections
Anchor Standards for Speaking and Listening: 4, 5
Anchor Standards for Writing: 6, 10

Final Assessment Option 3: Specifying Student Roles During Discussion

You can use discussion groups in your classroom for many different reasons. If you desire to "check in" on Standard 6 with students, you can use specific roles for students to increase feedback and focus on formal English and discipline-appropriate vocabulary. To use this assessment option, assign one person in each discussion group to be the "formal language checker." This person provides feedback in the moment to ensure that students use appropriate language. The teacher should circulate from group to group and collect data about student progress. Again, this is a more informal structure or practice; it's not necessarily an authentic performance task. Using this practice regularly can help you assess Standard 6 in your classroom.

Connections
Anchor Standards for Speaking and Listening: 1, 4
Anchor Standard for Reading: 1

Final Assessment Rubric Guidance

You may wish to adapt the rubric criteria in Figure 9.4 to fit the needs of your students and your situation. Only the highest level is provided in an effort to help you focus on the end goal as described by the standard.

Figure 9.4 Rubric Criteria

Rubric Indicator	A Description of Capstone Performance
Word Choice	• Speech includes discipline-specific language. • Speech includes vocabulary that is grade appropriate.
Pacing and Flow	• Speech is clear and at an appropriate pace. • Speech does not include any interruptions (such as yeah or um). • Speech is able to be repeated or rephrased clearly upon request.
Grammar	• Speech employs grade appropriate grammar and mechanics. • Speech uses a variety of interesting grammatical structures.

Suggestions for Differentiation

As this standard usually occurs in conjunction with other standards, there are many opportunities for differentiation. Students can practice this standard with increased frequency as needed. Some students may need additional practice to reach proficiency. (This is true of all standards, but especially this one!)

1. Provide students with additional opportunities to practice discipline-specific vocabulary or pacing without interruptions (such as ums). These practice opportunities can ensure that all students meet mastery at their own rate.
2. Have students use a voice recorder (smartphones are great for this) so they can listen to their speeches. This provides a powerful mechanism for student self-assessment. Listening to their own speech can be a very powerful way for struggling students to refine and improve their performance.
3. Students who are easily able to present with formal English can videotape themselves to start to focus on their formal presence in the room when they speak. Do they share their information while orienting their body forcefully toward the audience? Do they use

hand gestures and other body movements to present their message? Using the body in these ways can help take their formal speech to the next level.

4. Ask students to design their own differentiation. Hold them to a high standard of rigor.

Window Into the Classroom

Matt, an eighth-grade teacher was tired of students' informal language during both class discussion and formal presentations in his social studies class. Each year during the days leading up to Election Day, Matt helped his students uncover important principles about Roman government, culminating in an election debate between two Roman leaders. Matt wanted his students to practice formal language with greater emphasis throughout the unit as well as during the debate. Matt selected two learning activities (one of which was a differentiation option) to add to his instructional sequence. He also added Vocabulary Cartoon as a way for students to reinforce the formal vocabulary required the day before the election debate in his classroom. Consider the following sequence:

- ◆ **Learning Activity:** After students acquired basic facts about Roman democracy through a mini-lesson and analysis of two primary source documents, students used instaGrok to search three "big ideas" from the primary sources. Using the webbed diagrams from instaGrok, the students created a long list of formal words that might be needed during the unit of study. Working as a class, students sorted the words into tier 1, tier 2, and tier 3. Tier 2 words became words of emphasis.

- ◆ **Learning Activity:** Next Matt provided a series of mini-lessons on different issues within the Roman Empire. Using this knowledge, students began to prepare for their debates. Matt gave students digital recorders to practice their arguments. Students had to listen to their arguments and self-assess according to word choice, pacing and flow, and grammar.

- ◆ **Final Assessment:** Matt used Final Assessment Option 2, Vocabulary Cartoon, in conjunction with his debate assessment. First, students created vocabulary cartoons and presented them to a small group. Students used this as a final practice opportunity for using formal English right before the debate. After receiving feedback from their peers and the teacher on their cartoons and presentations, students conducted the assessment debate Matt had in his original design.

At the end of the learning experience, Matt observed a huge improvement in his students' abilities to share information formally and professionally. When students stated their arguments during the debate, they had increased confidence in delivering their message successfully.

However, Matt realized that he would have to maintain the expectation of formal speech in sharing and discussions throughout the year if he wanted the practice to become fully integrated into students' lives. He intended to require this type of speaking several more times throughout the school year.

Teacher Perspectives

For this instructional framework, two teachers across the United States adapted these ideas to their specific needs and situations. Read on to learn more about their experiences and successes.

I have many ESL students in my class, so I decided to try the tiered vocabulary strategy shared in this framework. As students encountered words they didn't know, they started labeling them as tier 1, tier 2, or tier 3. This helped them determine how important learning a particular word was. This strategy really helped me keep vocabulary instruction linked to students' needs.

—Jen, ESL Teacher

After reading this framework, I started doing Pinwheel Discussions every week. Students really liked that they were in control of the format. By making it a routine, I had time every week to engage students in academic conversation about a topic they had learned. It also gave students the opportunity to hear other students' perspectives more regularly. Great strategy!

—Amy, Third-Grade Teacher

Look Back and Step Forward

Speaking with clarity and poise augments the impact of one's message. Speaking in a way that garners respect can help students get jobs, share innovative ideas, and create positive change. Yeah, um . . . it's worth it!

 ## A Question to Consider as You Reflect

*How can students use words more strategically in
both formal and informal conversations?*

Other Great Tech Tools and Instructional Strategies That Didn't Make the Frameworks

There's More Out There

Hopefully the instructional frameworks shared in this text sparked many ideas and changes in your classroom about the ways you can promote both face-to-face and digital conversations. However, the instructional frameworks are far from exhaustive. Many great digital tools and instructional strategies didn't make the frameworks. Many of these resources are provided for you here. What will you do with these tools to fulfill the demands of the Common Core Speaking and Listening Anchor Standards?

Digital Resources

Google Voice

Google Voice is a free service provided by Google that connects to a Google e-mail account (also known as a Gmail account). With this service you can create a unique telephone number with special settings. Unless the telephone number is connected to a cell phone, calling the number will send the caller directly to voice mail. Every message that is left for the voice mail service is converted into a digital audio file (MP3 file) and saved in an online mailbox that can be accessed from anywhere. Google Voice also attempts to transcribe the message, but the transcriptions are often far from perfect (and sometimes hilarious). The digital recordings also can be linked to or embedded in websites. This allows teachers to easily record class discussions, student presentations, or homework assignments. To get started with Google Voice, follow these five steps:

1. Create a class Gmail account at mail.google.com. (Using this account only for school/class projects and purposes helps ensure that the mailbox is safe and appropriate for students to access.)
2. Go to voice.google.com.
3. Choose to have a new Google Voice Number attached to your account.
4. Set up other settings as you wish. (Record your message, etc.)
5. Give students the Google Voice Number, and have them call in to get started!

This tool works in any situation in which students may use the classroom phone or their cell phones to make calls either inside class or outside of class.

♦ A kindergarten teacher has students use the classroom phone to call the Google Voice Number to practice their fluency. Students read books, their writing journals, or poems with a partner. When they think they have "smooth reading," they call the Google Voice number from the classroom phone and read into the phone. The teacher listens to the recordings and puts them into digital folders inside Google Voice. At parent-teacher conferences or student meetings, the teacher plays the recordings to show growth in student fluency.

♦ A fourth-grade teacher uses her Google Voice number to monitor student conversations during literature circle groups. Because the teacher cannot participate in all the literature circle conversations at once, she has one student from each group call the class Google Voice number and put the phone on speakerphone. The teacher listens to the recordings and shares selected conversations with the entire class to model appropriate discussion techniques.

♦ An eighth-grade teacher occasionally offers students the option to "call it in" for a homework assignment. So instead of writing the answer to a question or series of questions at night, students call the Google Voice number and state their answers into the phone. The teacher reviews the recordings and embeds the best ones on the class blog. Students love listening to their peers via the site!

♦ A high school teacher uses the class Google Voice number to provide students with a way to get feedback on their end-of-the-year persuasive speeches. Students can call the number and record their speeches. Then the teacher downloads the audio file and posts it to the class website. Students can leave comments or ideas for the student. Students can access peer feedback on an as-needed basis. Some students note that they are able to make huge changes in the effectiveness of their speech delivery by using the system.

Vocaroo

Vocaroo is a new service that makes creating public, digital recordings easy for students. They can share their recordings on social media networks, blogs, and websites. The one thing that makes this service different from Google Voice is that all the recordings are public by default. Also, recordings are made using computers, not phones. To get started with Vocaroo, follow these four quick steps:

1. Go to vocaroo.com.
2. Have students press the record button, and record a message.
3. When students are satisfied with a message, they save it.
4. Have students use the social media buttons that appear to share a recording or use the embed code to put it on the class blog.

This tool is very easy to use, and it applies to all grade levels. Here are a few examples of how teachers across the country have used this tool:

♦ A first-grade teacher shares the tool with many of her parents who work. Instead of coming in to read books to the class, the parents record themselves on Vocaroo and send the link to the teacher. The teacher plays the recording for the class and then posts it to the class website. During literacy centers, students can continue to read virtually with their parents!

♦ A sixth-grade teacher has students post compliments about their classmates (no last names, of course) using Vocaroo. Students record compliments and post them in the comment section of other students' blogs. The sixth-grade teacher uses the activity around Valentine's Day so every student receives positive messages. The sixth-grade teacher also uses the activity to help students consider and deploy emotionally charged language when speaking and interacting with others.

♦ A high school teacher uses Vocaroo to have students who have difficulty writing or typing notes summarize the "big ideas" from a class orally. Each day the teacher posts the recordings to a page on the class website, and all students can use the recordings to help them review and study major concepts.

What's Going On in This Picture?

As the saying goes, sometimes a picture is worth a thousand words. This weekly blog series from the *New York Times* provides students and teachers with extremely interesting and unusual photographs snapped by *New York Times* photographers. Students are encouraged to have class or small-group discussions about the photos and then post their predictions to the site itself. About a week after the photo is first posted, the *New York Times* provides background information on the photo. This allows students to determine the actual accuracy of their predictions. To get started with What's Going On in This Picture?, follow these three steps:

1. Visit the site at learning.blogs.nytimes.com/category/lesson-plans/whats-going-on-in-this-picture/.
2. Preview the pictures posted to the site.
3. Select an image and present it to your students for discussion!

This site has images on it that would be suitable for all ages, but most of the images are geared toward middle school and high school students. Consider the following examples:

♦ A fourth-grade teacher uses a few pictures from this site to have her students practice group work at the beginning of the year. Then she asks students to bring in or e-mail their own pictures for other students to discuss at various points throughout the year. It ends up sparking a class tradition that fosters verbal vocabulary development!

♦ A seventh-grade teacher shows students one of these images every Friday. In groups, students discuss the photo and what it may mean. As they work, students are encouraged to use classroom and digital resources to find evidence to support their predictions. Students share their predictions with the class. Finally, the teacher reveals background information about the photo, and students self-evaluate their predictions in light of the new information.

♦ A high school teacher uses this site to create anchor activities that require meaningful conversation. If students finish a task or project early, the teacher has several posts from this site bookmarked on a student computer in the back of the room. Students discuss the images in pairs and try to discern the situation depicted in the photograph. It provides a great opportunity for students to engage in academic dialogue and problem solving.

StoryCorps iPhone App

StoryCorps (storycorps.org/iphone/) is an independent, nonprofit group on a mission to record and archive oral history in the United States and beyond. The organization provides a public service to people by allowing them to record their stories and having them archived in the Library of Congress. As part of its effort to collect as many oral histories as possible, StoryCorps has created an iPhone app that allows people to both listen to stories and share their own stories. This app is free, and it can be downloaded on iPhones, iPods, and iPads. The stories shared on the app are brief. (Most are under three minutes in length.) The app also includes step-by-step instructions for recording a story, prompting questions if inspiration is needed for a story, and integration with Twitter and Facebook so personal stories or the stories contained on the site can easily be shared. To get started with the StoryCorps iPhone App, follow these steps.

1. Go to the App Store on your iPhone, iPod, or iPad.
2. Search for StoryCorps.
3. Download the free app, and wait for it to install.
4. Begin listening to stories and recording stories!

StoryCorps has many different types of stories, and many are appropriate for all ages. However, it's always best for a teacher to preview the stories before sharing them with the class. Here are a few ways teachers are using StoryCorps:

♦ A third-grade teacher uses the app to help her students develop listening comprehension and empathy. Students listen to a story from the app about once a week. Then they discuss how the individuals in the story must have been feeling.

♦ A seventh-grade teacher has each student interview "an elder" and post the story to StoryCorps. The students are responsible for crafting important questions that capture and "explode" a single moment. Many students report that this is the best activity they've done during the entire year of school.

♦ A ninth-grade teacher uses this site as a way for students to analyze the power of inflection when speaking or recording their voices. Students listen to several different stories from the site and discuss what makes a narrator engaging or boring. From this experience, students list specific things that they will try to incorporate when they are speaking aloud in class or in life!

Instructional Strategies

List, Group, Label

List, group, label is a strategy that is applicable to any subject, and it stems from the idea that humans need to categorize and name their world to make meaning from it. However, if students talk, collaborate, and share during this activity, additional synthesis happens. It requires students to analyze text or media and then determine how the salient points of the content fit together. This strategy can be used with any content area and any grade level. Essentially, differentiation happens based upon the selection or topic that students use to "list, group, and label." Try these six steps to use this strategy in your classroom:

1. Begin by providing students with a reading selection, a general topic, a video clip, or an image.
2. Ask students to work in pairs or teams of three to read, view, or consider whatever you have provided for them. (You can certainly provide different groups of students with different content as appropriate.)
3. After considering the content carefully, students begin to brainstorm the ideas they learned. They should put down as many ideas as possible. Each idea should be recorded on its own sticky note or index card.
4. Next, students should reorganize all the ideas into groups. During this step, it is important to emphasize that students must verbalize to, and discuss their rationales with, one another as they work collaboratively to create groups from the single items.
5. Finally, students should determine a title for each group of ideas. It is helpful to have students create an entire sentence to label each category; however, you may want students to label using a single word. It really depends on the topic and your students. Again,

be sure to emphasize the need for students to discuss and justify their labels orally with all group members before recording them in writing.

6. Have students present their labeled groups to the class. Ensure that all students have the opportunity to ask the presenters questions about their thinking and rationale.

This strategy works well with students of any age or subject. It is extremely flexible, and it also is a great method to encourage conversations that use academic vocabulary. Consider the following ways that some teachers have used this strategy.

◆ A kindergarten teacher has students work in pairs to use this strategy after reading a book about butterflies. Students are encouraged to talk about their ideas, draw ideas, and write ideas on their sticky notes. Then, in pairs, they group the sticky notes and think of a name for the group. Students share their groups and labels with the class. The teacher puts adult writing on their documents where appropriate.

◆ A fourth-grade teacher uses this strategy to help her students determine the main ideas from their science and social studies texts. Students buddy read a selection or primary source document. Then they discuss the salient points, listing each one on a sticky note. Finally, they group and label their ideas. As students present to the class, the teacher emphasizes that there is no "right answer" regarding the main idea of a passage, but there are more precise and less precise answers. Students then vote on the most precise labels.

◆ A high school chemistry teacher uses this strategy to help students consider the reasons and rationales for the different groupings within the periodic table. Working in groups of four, students must list as many facts as they know about a set of elements provided to them by the teacher. From those facts, students must determine appropriate groupings. Students are encouraged to orally debate the placement of their information. Finally, students label each grouping and share their groupings with the class. Note that this activity is done *before* students are introduced to the formal categories contained within the periodic table. The activity itself allows students to create a context for acquiring that basic information.

Draw and Share

Draw and share is a method for students to process what they are learning orally and visually. The process is quick and informal, and it seeks to make students more comfortable explaining their ideas without the support of written papers or bulleted PowerPoint slides. Essentially, students are encouraged to process what they hear (either via video or a read-aloud) through sketches or drawings. Students must then present and explain their sketches to a small group or the entire class. It is a fast, simple way to have students meet the demands of the Common Core Standards for Speaking and Listening Anchor Standards. Try these four steps to use Draw and Share in your classroom:

1. Either play a video or read a text aloud that is relevant to your students and the content you teach.
2. As you read, have students individually sketch or doodle about what they are hearing.
3. After you have finished sharing the content with students, give students at least two to three minutes to organize their ideas and add any final touches to their sketches.
4. Have students share their sketches in pairs, small groups, or whole-group settings. Emphasize the need to maintain eye contact and not to stare at the sketch or image.

This simple strategy can be used in a variety of settings, and it simply provides teachers with a vehicle for students to practice speaking and listening without written prompts. Consider these examples.

♦ A second-grade teacher encourages her students to doodle as she reads a math problem aloud. Students then share their drawings with a peer. This form of processing helps students identify good strategies for solving the problem itself!
♦ An eleventh-grade U.S. history teacher has students listen to him read a recount of a Civil War battle. As they listen to the account, students sketch what is happening on the battlefield. Students share their ideas in small groups after the teacher is finished.

Save the Last Word for Me

Short, Harste, and Burke designed this strategy, and it is an excellent way to have students engage in a more formal discussion protocol. It can be used with any type of text in virtually any subject. It works best with students in grades 4 through 12 due to the multi-step nature of the strategy. The protocol allows students to independently prepare a reaction to a quote, facilitate a small-group discussion about the quote, and then summarize the experience. Try these four steps to use this strategy in your classroom:

1. Have students read a text in your subject area. (Primary sources work great with this strategy.)
2. Give students index cards.
   - On one side of the index card, have students write a favorite quote from the passage.
   - On the other side of the index card, have students write their reaction to the quote. You can give students such prompting questions as these: Why did you choose this quote? How does this information relate to you? Why is this important?
3. Students should join together in groups of three or four students.
4. Each student takes a turn facilitating the discussion. To facilitate the discussion, each student should do the following:
   - Read the quote he or she selected from the text.
   - Ask the group: Why do you think I chose this quote? How does this information relate to you? Why is this important?
   - The student facilitator should ensure that all students in the group have an opportunity to share.
   - Once everyone has shared, the student facilitator should share the insight recorded on the second side of their index cards. This gives the student facilitator the "last word."

This strategy works well with all content areas, and it encourages students to take an active leadership role in the discussion process. Here are some examples of teachers who use this strategy.

- A fifth-grade teacher uses this strategy when her class reads the novel *The Outsiders.* The students use this strategy to review each chapter after reading it. Because many students have connections to the text, the discussions become very passionate. Many students note that they especially enjoy being able to facilitate the discussion themselves.
- A seventh-grade social studies teacher uses this strategy to help students connect to current event articles they read. By discussing their personal connections to the events, students are more likely

to develop not only their speaking and listening skills but also their empathy!

♦ A tenth-grade teacher uses this strategy to help students understand primary sources they read. Because primary sources can be complex and multifaceted, having students discuss their takeaways at length can encourage rereading and increased comprehension.

 ## Step Back and Look Forward

As you navigate the demands of the new standards, continue to seek opportunities for your students to practice speaking and listening.

 ## A Question to Consider as You Reflect

Where are the best places to find resources? What is worthy of sharing with colleagues?

What's Next? Realistic Ways to Get Started

Moving Forward

You have reached the end of this book! As you read this sentence, you are most likely very excited and energized to emphasize authentic speaking and listening in your classroom.

However . . .

Reality and life will set in. You will have grades to submit, lesson plans to complete, and curriculum maps to follow. Integrating the Common Core Standards for Speaking and Listening Anchor Standards may drift from the forefront of your mind. So let's consider a few plans to help you implement the strategies in this text and shift your practice in ways that support students.

Make a Small Commitment

Start with a small commitment. Make that commitment *right now*. Don't begin by trying to implement all the frameworks, tools, and strategies in this book. Instead, choose one or two things to try *immediately*. To ensure that your commitment sticks, make a personal promise to share the results of your tiny classroom tests with a colleague, spouse, or friend. This will keep you accountable to your goals.

Stay Out of Crisis Mode

When deciding to implement a framework from this book, plan ahead. Ensure that you allot sufficient time to facilitate learning experiences that will allow students to meet the rigorous goals set forth in the framework. Crisis stifles innovation, so be sure to begin a framework calmly!

Experiment

As you begin to use some of the ideas contained within this text, be sure to experiment. In other words, personalize the tech tools and instructional strategies to meet the needs of your learners. Engaging in the design process is messy. Be tolerant of mistakes and failure along the way. Taking instructional risks is the only way to grow!

Collaborate

Find a colleague or friend who is willing to attempt some of the ideas within this book as you do. Given the growth of digital networks, this colleague can be across the hall or across the world. Once you've identified your partner, share your experiences with each other. This will help keep you focused and ensure that you receive timely feedback on your instructional designs and implementation.

Reflect

After you've tried a few ideas from this book, be sure to reflect on what you've accomplished. Such reflection is critical and allows you to engage in a cycle of continuous improvement.

In Closing . . .

Enjoy speaking and listening along with your students!

References

Alliance for Excellent Education. (2011). United States loses $5.6 billion providing college remediation [press release]. Retrieved from http://www.all4ed.org/press_room/press_releases/05052011

Archer, A. (2011). Vocabulary development [Web log post]. Retrieved from http://oregonliteracypd.uoregon.edu/topic/vocabulary-development

Beck, I., McKeown, M. G., & Kucan, L. (2002). *Bringing words to life: Robust vocabulary instruction.* New York, NY: The Guilford Press.

Beers, K. (2002). *When kids can't read: What teachers can do.* New York, NY: Heinemann.

Billmeyer, R. (2010). *Strategies to engage the mind of the learner: Building strategic learners.* New York, NY: Hawker Brownlow Education.

Bransford, J. D., Brown, A. L., Cocking, R. R., Donovan, M. S., & Pellegrino, J. W. (2000). *How people learn: Brain, mind, experience, and school.* Washington, DC: National Academies Press.

Geographical Association. (2009). Gapminder and world mapper [Web log post]. Retrieved from http://www.geography.org.uk/resources/gapminderandworldmapper

Hapgood, S., & Palinscar, A. S. (2006). Where literacy and science intersect. *Educational Leadership, 64*(4), 56–61.

Hattie, J. (2009). *Visible learning: A synthesis of over 800 meta-analyses relating to achievement.* New York, NY: Routledge.

Jessicaraba. (2012, December 2). @kristenswanson. Some questions: Is this just for fun, or does it meet my goal? Have students had a chance to try on their own/when should I? [Twitter post]. Retrieved from https://twitter.com/jessicaraba/status/275314883485118465

Joyce, B. & Weil, M. (1986). *Models of teaching.* Englewood Cliffs, NJ: Prentice-Hall.

Leithauser, B. (2012, November 21). *The box and the keyhole* [Web log post]. Retrieved from http://www.newyorker.com/online/blogs/books/2012/11/the-box-and-the-keyhole-two-ways-of-looking-at-fiction.html#ixzz2DGZusr47

Mandell, L. J. (2011, June 29). World's data doubles every two years, creating mega job opportunities [Web log post]. Retrieved from http://jobs.aol.com/articles/2011/06/29/worlds-data-doubles-every-two-years-creating-mega-job-opportunities/

Marzano, R. J. (2003). *What works in schools: Translating research into action.* Alexandria, VA: Association for Supervision & Curriculum Development.

MoniseLSeward. (2012, December 2). @kristenswanson. Are the outcomes clear? Is there more than one way for kids to show they've learned it? #ubdchat [Twitter post]. Retrieved from https://twitter.com/MoniseLSeward/status/275276169430044672

National Governors Association Center for Best Practices, Council of Chief State School Officers. (2010). Common core state standards for English language arts & literacy. Washington, DC: Author.

National Governors Association Center for Best Practices, Council of Chief State School Officers. (2012). About the standards. Common core state standards initiative. Retrieved from http://www.corestandards.org/about-the-standards

Palmer, E. (2012). Erik Palmer on the importance of speaking well. *ASCD Edge.* Retrieved from http://edge.ascd.org/_Erik-Palmer-on-the-Importance-of-Speaking-Well/video/1797015/127586.html#

Partnership for Assessment of Readiness for College and Careers. (2012). The PARCC assessment. Retrieved from http://parcconline.org/parcc-assessment

Perkins, D. (2010). *Making learning whole: How seven principles of teaching can transform education.* Hoboken, NY: John Wiley and Sons [Kindle edition].

Pottsedtech. (2012, December 2). @kristenswanson. I ask what parts of the goal I need to assess for prior knowledge, unpacking, dif't lessons for dif't minds #ubdchat [Twitter post]. Retrieved from https://twitter.com/pottsedtech/status/275277347945586688

Shanahan, T. (2012). The common core ate my baby and other urban legends. *Educational Leadership, 70*(4), 10–16.

Short, K. G., Harste, J. C., & Burke, C. (1996). *Creating classrooms for authors and inquirers.* Portsmouth, NH: Heinemann.

Smarter Balanced Assessment Consortium. (2012). Sample items and assessment tasks. Retrieved from http://www.smarterbalanced.org/sample-items-and-performance-tasks/

Spevack, J. (2012). NYC ischool gapminder [Web log post]. Retrieved from https://sites.google.com/a/nycischool.org/gapminder/about-gapminder-at-the-ischool

Steinhauer, J., & Schmidt, M. S. (2012, November 3). Man behind FEMA's makeover built philosophy on preparation [Web log post]. Retrieved from http://www.nytimes.com/2012/11/04/us/the-man-behind-femas-post-katrina-makeover.html?hp&_r=2&

Ujifusa, A. (2012, November 2). Scores drop on Ky's common core-aligned tests [Web log post]. Retrieved from http://www.edweek.org/ew/articles/2012/11/02/11standards.h32.html?tkn=QRCCNDb9WZ/A8pwmlYcfN7CfV7GiBt/wyeST&cmp=clp-sb-mw

Wiggins, G. (2011, November 17). The student voice: Our survey part 1 [Web log post]. Retrieved from http://grantwiggins.wordpress.com/2011/11/17/the-student-voice-our-survey-part-1/

Wiggins, G. (2012, Oct. 20). *Transfer and meaning making through UbD.* Paper presented at the UbD by the Seine Conference, Paris, France.

Wiggins, G., & McTighe, J. (2005). *Understanding by design* (2nd ed.). Alexandria, VA: ASCD.

Williamson, G. L. (2006). *Aligning the journey with a destination: A model for K–16 reading standards.* Durham, NC: MetaMetrics, Inc.